Fortune and Men's Eyes

FORTUNE
and Men's Eyes

by John Herbert

Grove Press, Inc.
New York

ACKNOWLEDGMENTS: "The Prisoner's Song" by Guy Massey, ©
copyright 1914 by Shapiro, Bernstein & Co., Inc., New York
USA, copyright renewed and assigned to Shapiro, Bernstein
& Co., Inc., reprinted by permission of Shapiro, Bernstein &
Co., Inc,; "A Good Man is Hard to Find" by Eddie Green, ©
copyright by Mayfair Music Corp., reprinted by permission
of Mayfair Music Corp.; "I'm A Big Girl Now" by Al Hoffman
& Milton Drake, © copyright 1946 by World Music, Inc., 18
East 48th Street, New York, N. Y. 10017, reprinted by special
permission of the publisher.

CAUTION: This play is fully protected, in whole, in part or in any
form under the copyright laws of the United States of
America, the British Empire including the Dominion of Can-
ada, and all other countries of the Copyright Union, and is
subject to royalty. All rights, including professional, amateur,
motion picture, radio, television, recitation, public reading,
and any method of photographic reproduction, are strictly
reserved. All inquiries should be addressed to the author's
agent, Ellen Neuwald, Ashley Famous Agency, Inc., 1301
Avenue of the Americas, New York, New York 10019.

First Evergreen Edition 1968
Eighth Printing 1980
ISBN: 0-394-17357-0
Grove Press ISBN: 0-8021-4304-0
Library of Congress Catalog Card Number: 67-31624

MANUFACTURED IN THE UNITED STATES OF AMERICA

DISTRIBUTED BY RANDOM HOUSE, INC., NEW YORK

GROVE PRESS, INC., 196 WEST HOUSTON STREET,
NEW YORK, N.Y. 10014

Fortune and Men's Eyes was first presented by David Rothenberg and Mitchell Nestor in association with The Little Room at the Actors Playhouse, New York, on February 23, 1967. It was directed by Mitchell Nestor, with setting by C. Murawski, costumes by Jan, and music and sound effects by Terry Ross. The cast was as follows:

ROCKY	Victor Arnold
MONA	Robert Christian
QUEENIE	Bill Moor
GUARD	Clifford Pellow
SMITTY	Terry Kiser

CHARACTERS

SMITTY: *A good-looking, clean-cut youth of clear intelligence and aged seventeen years. He has the look of a collegiate athlete. The face is strong and masculine with enough sensitivity in feature and expression to soften the sharp outline. He is of a type that everyone seems to like, almost on sight.*

ROCKY: *A youth of nineteen years who seems older and harder than his age should allow, though there is an emotional immaturity that reveals itself constantly. He has a nature, driven by fear, that uses hatred aggressively to protect itself, taking pride in harboring no soft or gentle feelings. He lives like a cornered rat, vicious, dangerous and unpredictable. He is handsome in a lean, cold, dark, razor-featured way.*

QUEENIE: *A large, heavy-bodied youth of nineteen or twenty with the strength of a wrestler but the soft white skin of a very blond person. Physical appearance is a strange combination of softness and hulking strength. For a large person he moves with definite grace and fine precision, almost feminine in exactness, but in no way frivolous or fluttery. Movements, when exaggerated purposely, are big, showy and extravagant. The face is dainty in features as a "cupie-doll's" . . . plump-cheeked and small-nosed. The mouth has a pouting, self-indulgent look, but the eyes are hard, cold, and pale blue like ice. The hair is fair, fine, and curly, like a baby's. One looks at him and thinks of a madam in a brothel . . . coarse, cruel, tough and voluptuously pretty.*

7

MONA: *A youth of eighteen or nineteen years, of a physical appearance that arouses resentment at once in many people, men and women. He seems to hang suspended between the sexes, neither boy nor woman. He is slender, narrow-shouldered, long-necked, long-legged, but never gauche or ungainly. He moves gracefully, but not self-consciously. His nature seems almost more feminine than effeminate because it is not mannerism that calls attention to an absence of masculinity so much as the sum of his appearance, lightness of movement, and gentleness of action. His effeminacy is not aggressive . . . just exists. The face is responsible for his nickname of "Mona Lisa." Features are madonna-like, straight-nosed, patrician-mouthed and sad-eyed. Facial contour is oval and the expression enigmatic. If he had been a woman, some would have described him as having a certain ethereal beauty.*

GUARD: *A rugged-faced man of about forty-five to fifty, who looks like an ex-army officer. He has a rigid military bearing, a look of order and long acquaintance with discipline. He presents an impressive exterior of uniformed law enforcement, but one senses behind the unsmiling features some nagging doubt or worry, as if something of his past returned occasionally to haunt him, when he would prefer it forgotten. At these moments, his actions are uneasy and he does not seem so impressive, in spite of the uniform. He has a stomach ulcer that causes him much physical discomfort, that manifests itself in loud belching.*

ACT ONE

SCENE ONE

Mid-October, evening.

*Overture: 3 songs—"Alouette" (sung by Group of Boys'
Voices); "Down in the Valley" (One Male Voice); "Jesus
Loves Me" (sung by Group of Boys' Voices).*

*A Canadian reformatory, prep school for the penitentiary.
The inmates are usually young, but there are often older
prisoners, as indicated by the dialogue in places. We are
primarily concerned here with four who are young, though
they tell us others exist. The overwhelming majority of
prisoners in a reformatory are in the late teens and early
twenties. Those who are older have been convicted of
offenses that do not carry a sentence large enough to
warrant sending them to a penitentiary. The setting is a
dormitory with four beds and two doorways. One door
leads to the corridor, but we do not see it. There is a
stone alcove, angled so that we get the impression of a
short hall. We hear the guard's key open this unseen door
whenever he or the four inmates enter or exit. The whole
upstage wall is barred so that we look into the corridor
where the guard and inmates pass in entrance and exit.
Another doorway leads to the toilet and shower room.*
ROCKY *is stretched on his bed like a prince at rest;* QUEENIE
sits on his own bed upstage; MONA *leans against the wall
of bars, upstage of* QUEENIE. *In the distance we hear the
clang of metal doors, and a gruff voice issuing orders.*
MONA *turns at the sounds, and looks along the hall.*

Just before lights come up, after curtain has opened, a BOY'S VOICE *is heard singing, at a distance—as farther along a corridor.*

BOY'S VOICE (*singing*):
Oh, if I had the wings of an angel
Over these prison walls would I fly—

Sound of metal doors clanging open and shut. And sound of heavy boots marching along corridor.

VOICE (*English accent*): Halt! Attention! Straighten that line! Guard! Take this one down and put him in Observation!

GUARD: Yes sir! Smith! Step out—and smartly!

Lights come up.

BOY'S VOICE (*singing*):
Oh, if I had the wings of—

QUEENIE (*on stage*):
Oh, if I had the wings of an angel,
And the ass of a big buffalo,
I would fly to the heavens above me,
And crap on the people below.

VOICE (*English accent; raised now, the voice is not only gruff as before, but high and shrill in overtone, like Hitler's recorded speech*): And you, Canary-Bird— shut that bloody row, or I shall cut off your seed supply.

Repeated sound of metal doors, and of boots marching away.

QUEENIE: Oh, oh! That's Bad Bess. The Royal Sergeant

don't come this close to the common folk, except when they're bringin' in a batch o' fish.

ROCKY: What's the action out there, Queenie?

MONA (*who stands nearest the bars*): It's the new arrivals.

ROCKY: Anybody ask you to open your mouth, fruity?

QUEENIE: Oh, lay off the Mona Lisa, for Christ sake, Rocky.

ROCKY: Always getting her jollies looking out that hole.

QUEENIE: Does Macy's bother Gimbel's?

ROCKY: They got their own corners.

QUEENIE: Well she ain't in yours, so dummy up!

ROCKY: Don't mess with the bull, Queenie!

QUEENIE: Your horn ain't long enough to reach me, Ferdinand.

ROCKY: You might feel it yet.

QUEENIE: Worst offer I've had today, but it's early.

ROCKY: Screw off! (*Turning toward* MONA.) Look at the queer watchin' the fish! See anything you can catch, Rosie?

QUEENIE: How's the new stock, Mona? Anything worth shakin' it for?

MONA: They're all so young.

QUEENIE: That'll suit Rocky. If he could coop a new chicken in his yard, he might not be so salty.

ROCKY: Where'd you get all that mouth . . . from your Mother?

QUEENIE: The better to gobble you up with, Little Red Riding Wolf!

ROCKY: Tell it to your old man.

QUEENIE: Which one? Remember me? I'm my own P. I.

ROCKY: You got a choice?

QUEENIE: I don't mean pimp, like you, I mean political influence, like me!

ROCKY: So you got a coupla wheels in the office! Big deal!

QUEENIE: I like it that way . . . makes it so I don't have to take no crap from a would-be hippy like you.

MONA: They're coming this way.

QUEENIE: Hell! And I didn't set my hair in toilet-paper curls last night. Oh well! I'll try to look seductive.

ROCKY: You better turn around then.

QUEENIE: Well, my backside looks better than your face, if that's what you wanta say.

ROCKY (*with disdain*): Queers!

Enter GUARD *with a youth who is about seventeen.*

ROCKY: Hi, screw! What's that . . . your new baby?

GUARD: You planning a return trip to the tower, smart boy?

ROCKY: Just bein' friendly, Captain! I like to make the kids feel at home.

GUARD: So I've noticed. (*To the new boy:*) Okay Smith, this is your dormitory for now. Try to get along with the others and keep your nose clean. Do as you're told, keep your bunk tidy, and no talking after lights out. You'll be assigned your work tomorrow. Meanwhile, follow the others to washup and meals. Pick up the routine and don't spend too much time in the craphouse, or you'll end up in an isolation cell.

ROCKY: He means Gunsel's Alley. Too bad all the queers don't make it there.

QUEENIE (*to the* GUARD): Now he wants a private room. Take him away, Nurse!

GUARD: Okay you two! Turn off the vaudeville. You'll get your chance to do your number at the Christmas concert. (*He exits.*)

QUEENIE: The Dolly Sisters! After you got your royal uniform, in the delousing room, did Bad Bess challenge you to a duel?

SMITTY: Who?

QUEENIE: Little Sergeant Gritt—that chalk-faced, pea-eyed squirt in the rimless goggles! He's always goin' on about the "Days of Empire" and "God and Country" and all suchlike Bronco Bullcrap.

SMITTY: Oh, yes! He did most of the talking.

QUEENIE: That's our Cockney cunt—never closes her hole. Didn't he want you to square off for fisticuffs, old chap? Sporting chance an' all that stale roast beef an' Yorkshire pudding?

SMITTY: Well, he did say he'd been boxing champion at some school in England, and that, if any of us thought we were tough, this was our chance to prove it—man to man, with no interference.

QUEENIE: Yeah—that's his usual pitch. Corny, ain't it? It

makes him feel harder than those stone lions out front o' Buckingham Palace. Yellow-bellied little rat! When he's outa that uniform, he's scared to death o' any eleven-year-old kid he meets on the street. Did his Lordship get any challengers?

SMITTY: Well, no! I wasn't surprised at that. I felt sure it was just a way of letting the prisoners know who's boss.

QUEENIE: I must say—you ain't exactly a idiot.

ROCKY: One o' these farty Fridays, he's gonna get it good, from some guy faster'n that goddam Indian.

QUEENIE: How stupid kin a Iroquois be? Imagine this jerky Indian from Timmins, takin' that fish-faced little potato chip at his word. The only one ever took the chance—far as I know.

SMITTY: He'd have to have a lot of guts.

QUEENIE: Oh yeah—and they showed them to him fast. He was a brave brave all right—an' stupid as a dead buffalo. The second he an' Bad Bess squared off at each other, two guards jumped Big Chief Running Blood, an' the three British bully boys beat the roaring piss outa him. Heroes all!

ROCKY: What a mess they made o' that squaw-banger!

QUEENIE: You couldn't exactly put that profile on a coin no more—not even a cheap little copper. Oh, well— let's look on the bright side o' the penny; he's in pretty good shape for the shape he's in. After all, he got a free nose-bob an' can pass for a pale nigger now. A darkie can get a better job 'n a redskin any day.

ROCKY: Whoever heard of a Indian what worked? They git government relief.

QUEENIE: Howdya think he got here, Moronia? He was one o' them featherheads from Matachewan Reservation, tryin' t' get a job in the mines. There was this great big ol' riot, an' the cowboys won again. Pocahontas' husband is up here because he tried t' scalp some Timmins cop. An', believe you me, that's the wrong way to get yourself a wig in that tin town.

ROCKY: An' you believe that crap, like he tells you his stories about how some stinkin' bird got its name? Jeez! Maybe you should git yerself a blanket an' become a squaw—you dig those tepee tales so much.

QUEENIE: I dig all kinds o' tail, pale-ass—except yours.

ROCKY: All Indians is screwin' finks an' stoolies, an' I woulden trust 'em with a bottle o' cheap shavin' lotion; and that Blackfeet bum probable slugged some ol' fairy in a public crapper, t' git a bottle o'wine.

QUEENIE: Always judgin' everybody by yourself! Tch! Tch! That's the sign of a slow con man, Sweetie.

MONA (*to new boy*): What's your name? I'm Jan.

SMITTY: Smith.

QUEENIE: But you can call her Mona, and I'm Queenie.

ROCKY: Look at the girls givin' the new boy a fast cruise. Give him time to take his pants off, Queenie.

QUEENIE: So you can get into them, Daddy-O? Don't let him bug you, Smitty. He thinks he's the big rooster here.

ROCKY: You know it too. Welcome home, punk!

SMITTY: This is my first time.

ROCKY: Braggin' or complainin'?

SMITTY: Neither. It's just a fact.

ROCKY: Well, that's nice. You shouldn't be here at all I guess. Got a bum beef?

SMITTY: A . . . a what?

ROCKY: Crap! A beef! A rap! Whose cookies did you boost . . . your mother's?

QUEENIE: What the judge wants to know, honey, is what special talent brought you this vacation . . . are you a store-counter booster or like myself do you make all your house calls when nobody's home?

SMITTY: Neither!

QUEENIE: Rolled a drunk . . . autographed somebody's checks . . . raped the girl next door . . . ?

SMITTY: No, and I . . . I don't want to talk about it.

QUEENIE: You might as well spill it, kid. I can't stand suspense. Ask Mona . . . she screwed all around the mulberry bush until I finally had to go find out in the office.

ROCKY: I coulda saved you the trouble and told you she reached for the wrong joy stick. Did you ever get one you didn't like, Mona?

MONA (*to* SMITTY): I've learned it doesn't matter what you've done. If you don't say, everyone assumes it's something far worse, so you might as well get it over with.

SMITTY: I just can't.

QUEENIE: OKAY Smitty . . . skip it! I'll find out on the Q. T., but I won't spill it.

ROCKY: Ottawa's First Lady! How did you do it, Ladybird?

QUEENIE: Well . . . I lifted my left leg and then my right, and between the two of them, I rose right to the top.

ROCKY: Of a pile of bull!

MONA: How long is your sentence?

SMITTY: Six months.

MONA: Same as mine. I have a few to go.

SMITTY: Does . . . does it seem as long as . . . as . . .

MONA: Not after a while. You get used to the routine, and there are diversions.

ROCKY: That's an invitation to the crapper.

MONA: Do you like to read?

SMITTY: I never did . . . much.

MONA: Well, this is a good place to acquire the habit.

ROCKY: Yeah! Let Mona the fruit teach you her habits, then you can go and make yourself an extra pack of weed a week.

QUEENIE: She don't go as cheap as you, Rocky. We're tailor-made cigarette girls or nothin'.

ROCKY: I get what I want without bending over.

QUEENIE: Sure! You can always con some stupid chicken into doing it for you. How many left in your harem now, Valentino?

ROCKY: My kids wouldn't spit on the best part of you.

QUEENIE: Who's interested in a lot of little worn-out punks? I've seen them all hustling their skinny asses in the Corner Cafeteria, and if it wasn't for the old aunties who feel them up in the show and take them for a meal, they'd starve to death. Did you tell them before they left that you'd provide them with a whole bus terminal to sleep in when you get out?

ROCKY: After I smarten them up, they don't have to flop in your hunting grounds. They go where the action is and cruise around in Cadillacs.

QUEENIE: Yours, of course?

ROCKY: What I *take*, you can call *mine*.

QUEENIE: What a pity you couldn't get a judge to see it the same way.

ROCKY: You're cruisin' for a bruisin', bitch!

QUEENIE: Thanks awfully, but I'm no maso-sissy, sad-ass. I always kick for the balls when attacked.

(*Sings to the tune of "Habanera" from* Carmen:)

My name is Carmen,
I am a whore,
And I go knocking
From door to door.

ROCKY: I'll meet you in front of the city hall next Christmas.

QUEENIE: Lovely, but don't ask me for a quarter, like last time.

ROCKY: Since when did you walk on the street with more than a dime?

QUEENIE: After I stopped letting bums like you roost at my place overnight.

ROCKY: Cripes! You'll never forget you played Sally Ann to me once. When you sobered up and felt like a little fun, did you miss me?

QUEENIE: . . . Yeah—also my marble clock, my garnet ring, and eleven dollars.

ROCKY (*laughing*): Oh jeez, I wish I coulda seen your face. Was your mascara running?

QUEENIE: He's having such a good time, I hate to tell him I like Bob Hope better. So where did you come from Smitty . . . the big corner?

MONA: That means the city . . . it's a slang term. You'll get used to them.

SMITTY: I feel like I'm in another country.

ROCKY: What's your ambition kid? You wanna be a Square John . . . a brown nose?

QUEENIE: Ignore the ignoramus. He loves to play the wise guy.

SMITTY: I'm willing to catch on.

QUEENIE: You will, but you gotta watch yourself . . . play it cool and listen to the politicians.

SMITTY: Politicians?

QUEENIE: The hep guys . . . hippos, who are smart enough to make it into the office. They get the best of it . . .

good grub, new shirts, and jeans, lightweight booties and special privileges . . . extra gym, movie shows, and sometimes even tailor-made cigarettes. Like to get in on that?

SMITTY: I don't smoke.

QUEENIE: Well for cripes' sake don't tell them. Take your deck of weed and give it to your mother.

SMITTY: My . . .

QUEENIE: Me, honey! Who else!

SMITTY: Oh! Okay!

MONA: Tailor-made cigarettes are contraband, but your package of tobacco is handed out with a folder of cigarette papers and a razor blade when you go for clothing change once a week . . . it's sort of a payday!

ROCKY: Listen to our little working girl. She works in the gash-house sewing pants together for the guys to wear. Her only complaint is there's nothing in 'em when they're finished.

SMITTY: Is that what I'll be doing . . . ?

QUEENIE: No baby, you won't. The tailor shop and the laundry are especially for us girls. They can make sure, that way, we don't stray behind a bush. But I like the laundry since they made me forelady. It's a sweet act of fate because it's the only place in the joint where I can get Javex—to keep myself a natural blonde.

ROCKY: And it's easier to show your ass bending over a tub, than under a sewing machine or a wheelbarrow.

QUEENIE: You've got a one-track mind, and it's all dirt.

ROCKY: My shovel's clean.

QUEENIE: I don't know how. Every time you get in a shower, you've got it in somebody's ditch.

ROCKY: Don't be jealous. I'll get around to shoveling in yours.

QUEENIE: Be sure you can fill it with diamonds when you come callin'.

ROCKY: You'd be happy with a fistful of chocolates.

QUEENIE: Feed the Lauras to your chickens at jug-up, eh Smitty?

SMITTY: Jug-up?

QUEENIE: Meals! Didn't they yell jug-up at you before you ate today?

SMITTY: I wasn't hungry. I thought the food would be the same as at the city jail, and it always made me sick after.

QUEENIE: Don't remind me of that sewage dump on the River. I think they bought that bloody old baloney and those withered wieners once a year . . . and you could put up wallpaper forever with that goddam porridge. Don't worry . . . the pigs they keep here are fed better than that.

MONA: Yes, the meals are good, Smitty. This place has its own farm, so the animals and vegetables are all raised by the prisoners.

SMITTY: I once worked on a farm, between school terms. I wouldn't mind if they put me on that . . . the time would go fast.

QUEENIE: That's the idea, honey! I'll try to wangle you a good go so you don't hafta do hard time. I got some pull in the office.

ROCKY: You'll have to serve a little keester to the politicians who wanna put you in the barn.

SMITTY: What?

ROCKY: But I guess you been in the hay before. Queenie's all for fixin' you up with an old man. You're ripe for tomato season.

QUEENIE: One thing about it, Rockhead. It'll be a hippy who's got it made, and no crap disturber like you that picks him off my vine.

SMITTY: I don't want to hurt anybody's feelings, but I'm not . . . queer. I've got a girl friend: she even came to court.

ROCKY: You shoulda brought her with you. I'da shared my bunk with her.

SMITTY: You don't understand, she's not that kind of . . .

MONA: It's all right, Smitty; he's just teasing you. Life inside is different, but you still don't have to do anything you don't want to, not if you—

QUEENIE: I'm tryin' to smarten him up, Mona, and you try to queer the play. Has sittin' outside the fence got you anything? At jug-up some punk's always grabbin' the meat off your plate and you're scared to say boo.

MONA: I get enough to eat. If anybody's that hungry, I don't begrudge it.

QUEENIE: And look at your goddam rags. They give you that junk on purpose, to make a bloody clown outa you. You ain't had a garment that fits since you come in.

MONA: I can fix them to look better at the shop when the guard's not looking.

QUEENIE: Well I like everything new. I can't feel sexy in rags.

MONA: I don't really care what I look like here.

QUEENIE (*sigh of despair*): See, Smitty! I try to sharpen the girls I like and she don't listen to a screwin' word I say. I coulda got her a real good old man, but she told him she liked her "independence" if you can picture it.

SMITTY: I can understand that.

QUEENIE: Yeah? So what happens? One day in the gym a bunch of hippos con her into the storeroom to get something for the game, and teach her another one instead. They make up the team, but she's the only basket. They all took a whack, now she's public property. You can't say no around here unless you got somebody behind you. Take it from your mother . . . I know the score.

SMITTY: I'll have to think about it.

QUEENIE: Well don't wait until they give you a gang splash in the storeroom. Mona had to hold on to the wall to walk, for a week.

MONA: They won't do it to him. He doesn't look gay, and he's probably not here on a sex charge. They felt I had no rights.

SMITTY: That doesn't seem fair.

MONA: I didn't think so either. It takes a while to get used to the rules of the game, and I've made a few concessions since . . . just to make life bearable. One thing, Smitty; don't depend on protection from the guards, and don't ever go to them. You have to solve your own problems.

ROCKY: And Mona'll show you her scars to prove it . . . fink! Squealed to a goddam screw! Cut you up pretty good after that, didn't we, bitch?

SMITTY: But how could they get away with it?

QUEENIE: The usual way . . . it was an "accident."

SMITTY: Jan?

MONA: Everyone agreed it was an accident . . . including me. Be careful, Smitty!

QUEENIE: Now Mona's givin' you some smart news. There's only two kinds of guards: the ones you can use like Holy Face who brought you in—and the fink screws that go straight to the General. When you see one comin' give six so we can play it safe.

SMITTY: Six?

QUEENIE: Say "six" instead of "nix" . . . a warning!

SMITTY: Oh, I get it.

QUEENIE: It's no game, Honey! They got a nice cold tower here with no blankets or mattresses on the iron bunks and a diet of bread and water to tame you. If that don't work, there's a little machine that fastens your hips and ankles, while some sad-ass screw that's got a rod on for you bangs you across the ass with a leather belt fulla holes, and some other son of a bitch holds your arms over your head, twisted in your shirt. They can make you scream for God and your mother before they let you go.

SMITTY (*aghast*): It sounds like the late late show.

QUEENIE: It's no Hollywood horror-vision. Ask Mona; she was in a fog for a month after.

SMITTY: Mona? . . . Jan?

MONA: I don't want to talk about that, Smitty.

ROCKY: No. She'd rather dream about it.

QUEENIE: She wakes the whole place in the middle of the night with those bloody awful screams—"Mother! Mother!" Crap!

SMITTY (*petrified*): You're only trying to scare me . . . all of you.

MONA (*gently*): No, we're not, Smitty . . . someone's always waiting for you to make a misstep. Please be careful.

SMITTY: I've heard of lashes, but I thought it was only in very special cases.

MONA (*bitterly*): They don't keep those little goodies because they have to but because they want to. Learn to look into their eyes before you stick out a hand.

SMITTY: Thanks, Mona, I'll remember.

QUEENIE: Well, now we're gettin' someplace. You see what a wise girl Mona's gettin' to be? She'll know the ropes better than me next time around.

SMITTY: Same thing happen to you?

QUEENIE: Well not exactly, but then I handle myself a little different. Mona's a girl who's gotta learn the hard way. I always see the trap before it springs. But then I have the advantage of early training. I was a Children's Aid ward, and shuffled around from foster homes to farms, to God knows what. I been locked in closets so my foster mother could drink and play cards unseen; I had farmers treat me worse'n their dogs, and I learned before I was twelve that nobody gives a crap about you in this cruddy world. So I decided to do something about it. Queenie looks after Queenie, and pretty good too let me tellya.

SMITTY: Sounds like you've had a rough time.

QUEENIE: Skip it! I wouldn't trade places with any soft son of a bitch who needs a goddam mother to tell it what to do and a lousy house in some phony suburb with home-baked pies, and a lot of chitchat around a kitchen table. I've seen what that does to people, and I hate them gutless bastards who go to work eight hours a day, to parties and shows the rest of the time, and walk around with their noses in the air like their own crap don't stink.

MONA: Queenie's never been able to find her mother. The Children's Aid wouldn't give the address because of her criminal record.

QUEENIE: Who wants it anyway? She's probably a pukin' prostitute somewhere, walkin' around the street with a gutful of gin. What dirty bitch would leave a kid before its eyes was open to be pushed around by a buncha bastards who only want some sucker to do the housework for them? I bailed myself outa that

crap when I was lucky thirteen and found out somebody liked my body. I been renting it out ever since.

ROCKY: But the offers are gettin' fewer and the rates are
gettin' lower. Next year you'll be dishwasher at the
corner lunch.

QUEENIE: Listen, asshole, as long as there's houses fulla
jewelry an' furs, this girl's hands will help to keep the
insurance companies in business, and don't you forget
it. It's you stinkin' pimps who better move fast an'
get it made before your hair an' teeth rot out on the
sidewalk. I'll wave at your bench as I ride past the
park in my limousine.

MONA (*seeing the* GUARD *approach*): Six!

Enter the GUARD *called "Holy Face."*

GUARD: Book-up! Okay Curlylocks, it's your turn to wheel
the library around, I'm advised from the office, so
try not to spend too much time visiting your friends
en route . . . everybody's entitled to a book, too.
Your pram's in the corridor.

QUEENIE: Thanks Daddy-O, I'll save you a Baby Bunting
book.

QUEENIE *combs his hair in preparation for the ex-
cursion.*

GUARD: We have another nice little detail in the V.D.
ward. A new patient just puked all over his cell, but
he's too weak to mop it up.

MONA: The poor kid!

GUARD: Okay, beautiful. I figure even you might be trusted
up there.

QUEENIE: Always the little mother, but don't go giving any kisses till he's had his shots, Nurse. (QUEENIE *exits, passes in corridor wheeling library cart.*) Cigars, cigarettes, vaseline! Everything for the home!

ROCKY: Thanks Captain! I was just about to bash their heads together when you made the scene. You saved me a trip to the tower.

GUARD: It's temporary, believe me. You've been getting closer to it every day. Don't start brooding, Smith . . . that doesn't help in here. Get yourself a book or something before lights out.

SMITTY: Yes sir.

ROCKY: My, my! What a polite little chap. Isn't he sweet, Officer?

GUARD: Lay off him Tibber, or I'll have you moved to a stricter dormitory. Can't you get along anywhere?

ROCKY: Sure, outside!

GUARD: Is that why we're honored by your presence so often?

ROCKY: Well the law don't like to see a smart guy get ahead. They want suckers who'll take a few cents a week, a row of brass buttons, and call it a living.

GUARD: But we can walk home when the work's done without an armed escort. Think about that, big shot!

ROCKY: I'm thinkin'. (*Gives the* GUARD *a look that seems to make the* GUARD *uneasy.*) You wanta stay nice an' honest—and keep it that way. Like, I mean next year ya kin take off wit' yer pension, ain't it? That is —if nothing don't go wrong.

GUARD: Lights out at eight o'clock, Smith! Be ready for bed by then.

SMITTY: Eight?

GUARD: That's right. You're up at six. It won't seem so early when you get used to the idea that, in the evening, there's no place to go.

SMITTY: I guess so.

GUARD: Okay, Florence Nightingale—on the double! (*Exits with* MONA.)

ROCKY: Oh boy! That sucker's ulcer's gonna kill'im afore he gits the chance t' sit at home in a rockin' chair.

SMITTY: He sure did look sick when he went out.

ROCKY: He's sick an' he makes me sick. You ain't smart, ya know, Smitty!

SMITTY: How come?

ROCKY: Fruits always get ya in the deep crap.

SMITTY: I don't know; I never knew any before.

ROCKY: You ain't been around.

SMITTY: No, I guess not.

ROCKY: They'll screw you up every time.

SMITTY: How?

ROCKY: 'Cause they're all phonies . . . gutless; they're all finks.

SMITTY: You sound like you've had experience with them.

ROCKY: An overdose! But no more! I gotta get me one when I get outa the joint. I'm gonna break both her legs . . . then I'm gonna put a coupla sharp chicks out on the hustle for me. That's the real dough.

SMITTY: You mean . . . women?

ROCKY: Let me tell ya! They were fallin' all over Rocky for me to be their boy, but I latched on to this one homo first to make a fast buck. Took him for everything he had . . . almost!

SMITTY: The homo?

ROCKY: Fag!

SMITTY: Oh—queer.

ROCKY: More money than bloody brains! Crazy about me! Old man's a big shot millionaire—stock exchange, race horses—the whole bit, but his one son was real fruit. It took some connin', but I got in solid . . . weekly allowance, swell apartment, lotsa booze and company and a Cadillac convertible.

SMITTY: All yours?

ROCKY: Except the heap! That's how she got me. I was browned off with the freak and split. Sold the works . . . television set, cut-glass decanters and whisky glasses, paintin's and statoos . . . all that crap! I split in the Caddy with a roll would choke a elephant an' had me a ball . . . hotel rooms an' motels from Montreal to Windsor . . . Forty-two street, Frisco . . . dames, cards, booze! Man, was I livin' high!

SMITTY: Money run out?

ROCKY: Hell no! When ya got it, ya can always make it, but that fruit had the brass to call the bulls and get me picked up for takin' the Caddy.

SMITTY: Because it wasn't yours?

ROCKY: What I take is mine—that's my motto. But those queers always like one string to keep ya in line. This bastard kept the car in her name so she could screw me up when the time came.

SMITTY: So he . . . she laid a charge?

ROCKY: Hell, no! She wanted me back, that's all. We agreed on a story to cover all the crap stirred up, but her old man and the bulls stepped in anyways and fixed me good. They tried to throw the book at me. Now, I'm gonna fix her, an' when I'm finished she won't be able to cruise no more little boys for about a year, except out a window or on a stretcher!

SMITTY: If you do that, maybe they'll send you back again.

ROCKY: You sure are dumb. After you do a job, like I'm gonna, on somebody, they're scared crapless . . . glad to give ya both sides o' the street. Never let a fruit scare ya . . . the cops don't like them either, so underneath they're yellow as a broken egg. Don't ever forget that.

SMITTY: I'll remember.

ROCKY: Ya know, I could make a real sharp guy outa you. Ya got a head an' ya don't shoot your mouth too much.

SMITTY: I don't know too much.

ROCKY: You'll learn, kid! You'll learn. Listen to old Rocky an' you'll get to sit on the sunny side of the yard. See . . . I'm in this dormitory because I raise hell a bit. That's why they put me with these two fruits—to watch me. But there's bigger an' better dorms with more guys, an' that's where I'll be goin' back to . . . an' so could you, if you play along with Rocky.

SMITTY: How do you mean?

ROCKY: Well ya gotta have a buddy, see? Ya can't get chummy with the whole joint, an' specially no fruits. If ya get that name, your ass is cooked when you get to a good dorm. Why d'ya think I give 'em a hard time here? If you're smart, you'll do the same thing. There's real guys in some corridors, so ya wanna keep your nose clean.

SMITTY: I sure don't want anybody to think I'm queer.

ROCKY: Good! That's what I like t' hear.

SMITTY: Why would they put me in this particular dormitory, I wonder? To watch me, too?

ROCKY: Ya musta done somethin' goofy before your bit here . . . took a poke at a copper or somethin' like that. They won't leave ya in here if Rocky can swing somethin' for us. The other blocks are probably filled up, but we'll be movin' soon. Would you go for that, kid?

SMITTY: Maybe it would be better.

ROCKY: Stick with the Rock an' you'll be looked up at. That ain't easy in the joint. Every jerk's lookin' for your jelly-spot. I didn't get the name I got by takin' it off these goons. Even the screws step easy on me. See how I talk to Holy Face? His blood turns to crap around Rocky.

SMITTY: He doesn't seem to stop you too much.

ROCKY: Nobody stops this boy. Besides I got somethin'
on Holy Face. I'll tell you if you make up your mind
who your buddy's gonna be. Remember what happened to Mona. You're sittin' duck for a gang splash
if y'ain't got a old man. I'm offerin' to be your old
man, kid, an' if you're wise you'll think fast. Whadda
ya say?

SMITTY: Would it keep me from . . . what happened to
Mona . . . in the storeroom?

ROCKY: Ya wouldn't want all those goons to pile on ya,
would ya, now?

SMITTY: No . . . for God's sake, no!

ROCKY: Am I your old man then?

SMITTY: Like . . . a buddy, you mean?

ROCKY: Sure, that's the score. I'll kill any son of a bitch
lays a hand on ya.

SMITTY: Okay . . . and . . . thanks!

ROCKY (*tossing* SMITTY *his cigarette lighter*): Here's a firebox for ya, kid. Keep it! We're gonna get along good,
Smitty. Ya wanna know what I got on Holy Face?

SMITTY: Well, sure!

ROCKY: He took a pigeon outa the joint for a pal o' mine,
so I know all about it, an' he knows I got the goods
on him. I throw him a hint every once in a while when
he thinks he's gonna push me around.

SMITTY: A pigeon?

ROCKY: A letter . . . a message! Jailbird lingo for stuff that
ain't allowed—(*with a confiding wink*) like a punk

kid is a chicken an' if he gives ya a kiss, that's a
bluebird. Everythin' you write's gotta go through a
censor in the office, but if ya got somethin' goin' for
ya, ya can allays buy some screw. One o' my buddies
gave Holy Face fifty bucks t' get a pigeon out for
him. That's about as much dough as a lousy screw
makes in a week, an' Holy Face ain't so holy as he
acts when it comes to makin' hisself a buck.

SMITTY: But there's no money in here. They kept mine at
the office.

ROCKY: You're green, kid. There's all kinds of lines goin'
around the joint.

SMITTY: But how?

ROCKY: Easy! Some relative calls in for a Sunday visit,
slips Holy Face the dough, an' next chance he's got,
he divvies up, takes out his half-C note and posts
your pigeon.

SMITTY: Why not get the relatives to take a message for
nothing?

ROCKY: There's things some relatives won't do. This was
a junk deal . . . dope . . . big-time stuff!

SMITTY: What kind of excuse could you give to ask fifty
dollars from a relative . . . here?

ROCKY: Plenty! Tell 'em the meals are crap an' cash could
get ya candy, magazines, or nice face soap . . . some
story like that. Say ya can only get stuff through a
good-hearted screw who's takin' a chance for ya.
Play it hearts an' flowers . . . works good on most
relatives.

SMITTY: I guess so.

ROCKY: So come on, baby, let's me an' you take a shower before bedtime.

SMITTY: A shower?

ROCKY: Sure! I like one every night before lights out!

SMITTY: Go ahead! I had one this afternoon when they brought me in and gave me a uniform.

ROCKY: It ain't gonna kill ya t' take another. I like company.

SMITTY: Tomorrow, Rocky.

ROCKY: Right now!

SMITTY: No . . . thanks!

ROCKY: I like my kids clean.

SMITTY: I'm clean.

ROCKY: Get up!

SMITTY: What . . .

ROCKY: Get movin' . . . into that shower room.

SMITTY: Rocky, you're not . . .

ROCKY: I said *move*, boy!

SMITTY: No! I changed my mind. I don't want an old man.

ROCKY: You got a old man, an' that's better than the store-room, buddy boy!

SMITTY: I'll take a chance.

ROCKY: I'll make sure it's no chance. It's me or a gang

splash. Now move your ass fast. I'm not used to punks tellin' me what they want.

He grabs Smitty's arm, twisting it behind the boy's back. SMITTY *gives a small cry of pain, but* ROCKY *throws a hand over his mouth, pushing him toward the shower room.* SMITTY *pulls his face free.*

SMITTY: Rocky . . . please . . . if you like me . . .

ROCKY: I like you . . . an' you're gonna like me!

Blackout

ACT ONE

SCENE TWO

Three weeks later, evening.

As scene opens, SMITTY *and* MONA *are lying or sitting on their own cots, each reading his own book.* ROCKY *can be heard off-stage, singing in the shower room.* QUEENIE *and the* GUARD *are both absent.*

ROCKY (*singing*): Oh, they call me The Jungle King, The Jungle King . . . (*Shouting.*) Hey-y—Smitty!

SMITTY: Yeah? (*Continues reading.*)

ROCKY (*off-stage*): Hey, Smitty!

SMITTY: Yeah, Rocky?

ROCKY (*off-stage*): Roll me some smokes!

SMITTY: Okay, okay. (*He moves, still reading, to Rocky's cot, where he finds package of tobacco, but no papers.*)

ROCKY (*still off-stage and singing*): Oh, the Lion and the Monkey . . .

SMITTY: What you got there, Jan? You must have had thirty takeouts in three weeks.

MONA: It's a book of poems.

SMITTY: Any good?

MONA: Yes, but it's not exactly what I wanted.

37

SMITTY: I've got something better; well, more useful, anyway. Come here; have a look.

MONA (*after crossing to join* SMITTY *on Rocky's bed*): "Advanced Automobile Mechanics." Very practical!

SMITTY: I'm a practical guy. You see, I figure I might not be able to get a job in an office, because—well—bonding, and all that. You know what I mean. Anyway, I worked evenings after school and all day Saturday in my fath—in a garage. I learned a lot about car motors, so I might as well put it to use. Mechanics are paid pretty good, you know.

MONA: That's wonderful, Smitty. This way, your time won't be wasted. You can make your six months really tell, and then after . . .

ROCKY (*entering singing and combing his hair*): The Jungle King, the Jungle King . . . Say-y! Whadya call this here scene—squatters' rights? Let me tellya somethin'—quick! In good ol' Cabbage-town, there's a li'l joint where me gang hangs out; it's called the Kay Won Cafe. Guess who runs it?

SMITTY: A Chinaman?

ROCKY: Wrong! Charlie owns it, but Rocky runs it. A pretty-boy comes in there 'n' I don't like his face much—me boys wait fer 'im outside, an' grab aholt his arm 'n' legs, an' Rock, who's welterweight champ 'round there, changes the smart guy's kisser a li'l.

SMITTY: You don't like your punching bag to swing too free. Your toughs have to hold him, eh?

ROCKY: I do things *my* way. There's another spot, on the

roughest corner in town, called Eddie's Poolroom. Now—guess who runs it?

SMITTY: Eddie?

ROCKY: Oh boy, do you learn slow! Same story. Eddie owns the shack, but ya kin bet yer sweet billiard cue The Rock says who's behin' the eight ball 'round there.

MONA (*rising from Rocky's bed*): All right, Rocky—I get the point.

ROCKY: Ya better see it, Pinhead—or I'll give ya a fat eye t' wear. Now beat it!

SMITTY: Leave him alone.

ROCKY: Oh, you ain't talkin' t' me.

SMITTY: Just don't touch him.

ROCKY: Whadya think he is—precious—or somethin' ?

SMITTY: Lay off, that's all.

ROCKY: How come ya talk t' me like that? Ain't I good t'ya, kid? Don't I getya cookies outa the kitchen? An' rubber t' chew, off Holy Face?

SMITTY: You're so good to me—and I'm so sick of it all.

ROCKY: Now, now! That ain't a nice way t' talk, when I just bin fixin' it up wit Baldy t' git us in "D" Dorm. Ain't that whatya wanted all along?

SMITTY: Let's not overdo this "togetherness."

ROCKY: Sad—sad—sad! We-ell—I guess I'll just hafta 'range us a li'l extra gym, so's ya don't feel too neglected. The boys'll wanna meet ya before we move inta their

Big Dorm. Tomorrow afternoon, Smitty? Get together wit de gang—just like at Eddie's or the Kay Won?

SMITTY: No, Rocky—no!

ROCKY: No what? No ketchup or no applesauce?

SMITTY: No—no extra gym.

MONA: Please, Rocky—we were only . . .

ROCKY: Shut up, ya wall-eyed whore!

MONA: I only . . .

QUEENIE *is heard singing, approaching in corridor.*

SMITTY: Six! Six! Forget it!

QUEENIE (*off-stage, singing*):
I'm a big girl now,
I wanna be handled like a big girl now;
I'm tired a stayin' home each evenin' after dark,
Tired a bein' dynamite without a spark . . .

Let me in. (*Stamping his feet.*) Let me in this cell!

QUEENIE *and the* GUARD *called Holy Face enter,* QUEENIE *carrying a small, white, cone-shaped Dixie cup. He continues singing.*

I wanna learn what homos do in Old Queen's Park . . .

GUARD: I wanna learn what you do up in that hospital so often.

QUEENIE: I show the surgeon my stretch marks.

GUARD: I know it can't be only for that coneful of cold cream. I'll bet if I gave you a frisk, I'd find scissors or a scalpel tucked in the seam of your shirt. I oughta search you every time out.

QUEENIE (*throwing open his arms*): Oh do, Daddy-O! I just can't wait t' feel your big callous hands on m' satin-smooth bode-ee!

GUARD: I'd as soon have syphilis.

QUEENIE: Who's she? Any relation to Gonorita?

GUARD: Cut it! Let's have a little common decency.

QUEENIE: What's that—somethin' ya eat? Ya know, you're not well at all; the way you been belchin' an' turnin' green around here lately. Maybe that ulcer of yours has soured into cancer, an' you'll never make that first pension check.

GUARD: I'll live to collect it all, and my stomach will sweeten considerably next winter, when I'm down in Florida—away from you bunch of bums. (GUARD *belches loudly.*)

QUEENIE: Pardon *you*! Will the rest be up in a minute? Maybe if the Doc finds out you ain't fit to work, they'll fire ya. Part-pension won't pay the shot for Palm Beach.

GUARD: One thing—I'm going to find out what you do with all those gobs of goo from the dispensary. I suspect it's got somethin' to do with the backside of decency. (GUARD *exits to shower room.*)

QUEENIE: How gross of you, Gertrude. No secret at all! I mix the cold cream with coal dust off the window sills, an' sell it to the screws for mascara. Helen Roobenbitch ain't got nothin' on me. (*Exits to shower room. Sound of a slap. Off-stage:*) Brutality! Brutality!

GUARD (*entering*): Next stop for that one is the bug wing.

It might as well wear its jacket the same way it does everything else—backwards!

ROCKY: Take it an' tie it up an' don't never ever bring it back no more.

GUARD: Okay. Book-up time. Anybody want a trip to the library?

ROCKY: Yeah! I'll take a book o' matches—t' the works.

GUARD: Pyromania would become you, Tibber; you got all the other bugs.

ROCKY: It bugs me watchin' noses stuck into sheets o' paper day 'n' night. Ain't that right, Smitty?

GUARD: Keep right on reading, Smith! There's no safer pastime around here. Tibber never got past Super-Rat. Well—if that's it, I'll head for a smoke in the lock—

MONA: I'd like to go to the library.

GUARD: Again? You're there every time the doors open. Can't you wait for the cart to come around?

MONA: It won't have what I'm looking for.

GUARD: Cripes! If there wasn't bars on that book room, you'd be breakin' in.

MONA: Mr. Benson said that I could find something to do for the Christmas concert. (*Shows* GUARD *library pass-card.*)

GUARD: I thought Benson ran the orchestra. Why don't he get you to play the skin flute?

ROCKY: Yah! Yah! The Minnie-Lousy could give him lessons.

MONA: Mr. Benson's in charge of drama for the concert, too. I'm going to do something like that.

GUARD: Why don't you do "I'm A Big Girl Now"? Sassy-face in there could teach you the words.

MONA: I don't sing.

GUARD: Oh, hell! Come on, Hortense; your carriage awaits without.

MONA: Thank you.

SMITTY: See you after, Jan.

MONA: See you, Smitty.

GUARD *and* MONA *exit.*

ROCKY (*singing introduction to "I'm A Big Girl Now"*):
Me 'n' my chilehood sweetheart
Ha' come t' de partin' o' de ways . , .

SMITTY: Oh, you're really funny.

QUEENIE (*entering from shower room singing*):
He still treats me like he did
In our bab-ee days,
But I'm a little bit older
And a little bit bolder
Since both of us were three . . .

ROCKY: Put down that bloody book, kid!

SMITTY *does so, and sits looking at* ROCKY.

QUEENIE (*still singing*):
I'm a little more padded
Somethin' new has been added . . .

ROCKY: I got best bunk in this joint; can see everything

comin' at us down the hall. I wantya t' know I'm real particular who uses it. That thing don't sit on my bunk no more.

SMITTY (*rising*): That'll make two of us . . .

ROCKY (*pushing him back*): What's mine is yours, kid.

QUEENIE: An' what's urine is my-yun.

SMITTY: Keep it! I only want what's mine. (*He gets up again and goes to lie face down on his own cot.*)

ROCKY: Come again on them mashed potatoes.

SMITTY: You heard me.

ROCKY: Watchit! I warned ya 'bout the tomato sauce. Be a good kid now, an' roll me a smoke.

SMITTY *casually rolls a cigarette, as though it is second nature to do so for* ROCKY.

QUEENIE: And when you've done that, Cinderella—mop the floor, wash the windows, shake the rugs and . . .

SMITTY: Aw, cut it, Queenie!

ROCKY: Smitty likes to keep the old man happy, don't you, kid?

SMITTY: Sure!

QUEENIE (*Singing to tune of "Old Man River"*):
Far far be it from me to free the slaves;
I'm not honest, and my name ain't Abe.
He just keeps rollin'-rollin' those ciggie-boos.

ROCKY: Yer name'll be mud if you keep that up.

QUEENIE: Queen Mud to you, peasant!

ROCKY: I think she's jealous, Smitty.

QUEENIE: Of what, for crap's sake?

ROCKY: 'Cause me an' Smitty is such good buddies. Bugs you, don't it?

QUEENIE: I don't give a damn if you legalize it in church-up next Sunday, and have fourteen babies. It ain't green you see in my eye, it's red, 'cause I hate to see a guy who could be a hippo playin' bumboy to a haywire loony who'll get him an ass-beat or a trip to the tower before his time's up.

ROCKY: You're really askin' for it, ain't ya?

QUEENIE: I'd like nothin' better than for you to take a swing at me, rockhead. Then we'll see who's gonna be called mud!

ROCKY: I'll find a better way, and you can believe it.

QUEENIE: It'll have to be while I'm asleep, 'cause I can see your next move like you drew me a map.

ROCKY: How come you're so smart . . . for a queer?

QUEENIE: 'Cause I get to bed bright an' early, and I'm up with the jailbirds—fresh as a pansy! We can't all be as dumb as you, Dora; it makes for bad publicity.

ROCKY: When you find me underneath, class me with you. For right now you call me Mister!

QUEENIE: How'd you like to say hello to your dear old friend, Baldy, in the office? He tells me he knows you from your first semester here, when you were chicken, like Smitty. I believe he gave your coming-out party, and made you debutante of the year.

ROCKY: I ain't interested in no old fairy's tales.

QUEENIE: May I quote you, or don't you want Baldy to pick you out a nice private room, where you can count your bellybutton and say your prayers, to pass the time?

ROCKY: Shoot off your mouth any way you want. Baldy an' me get along just fine.

QUEENIE: Yeah, he's got a soft spot in his head for you . . . except when he sees Smitty. Your sonny outshines you, it seems.

ROCKY: If he likes me, he's gotta like my buddy too.

QUEENIE: He does. Oh yes indeedy, *how* he does!

SMITTY: Why don't you two turn it off? What am I anyways, a piece of goods on the bargain counter?

QUEENIE: That's up to you, honey. If you smartened up, you could be as high-priced as you want.

SMITTY: I just don't want to be bugged, that's all. Let me do my time the easy way.

QUEENIE: Like the Mona Lisa?

SMITTY: What's Mona got to do with it?

QUEENIE: Well, she don't believe in wheelin' an' dealin' either, and you see what she gets. You gotta hustle inside too, you know, or you end up like a chippy-ass, wipin' up somebody's puke.

SMITTY: I thought you were Mona's friend.

QUEENIE: I am, and I guess I like her 'cause she's different from me. But that don't mean a comer like you has got to settle for the crappy end of the stick. You could have it all your own way . . . by just reachin' for it. You can't park your keester in a corner 'round here.

SMITTY: I'm satisfied to sit it out.

QUEENIE: Okay. Play it safe, but don't be sorry later. Nobody'll bother you while you got a old man, but you'll be anybody's baby when he drops you for a new chicken.

ROCKY *sings first two lines of "Jalousie."*

QUEENIE: It's Catso-Ratso, your old gearbox buddy who's got the greenies. That Wop's gonna get you good.

ROCKY: No Macaroni scares me, sister!

Sound of metal door opening and closing at a distance.

VOICE (*at distance, along corridor*): Tower up!

SECOND VOICE: Tower screw!

THIRD VOICE (*closer*): Hack from Tower!

FOURTH VOICE: Holy Face with hack!

FIFTH VOICE (*near-by*): Who they after?

SIXTH VOICE (*next cell*): They're still comin'. Must be after Rocky! (*Same.*) Hey Rocky! What'd ya do now?

GUARD (*off-stage*): Shut those goddam traps!

VOICE (*at distance*): Holy Face is a stinkin' lush.

On-stage cell inmates pick it up.

ROCKY: Beats his wife an' bangs his daughter.

QUEENIE: Not our Holy Face! He does it on his dear ol' granny.

GUARD (*off-stage*): Who in hell said that?

A short silence.

VOICE (*at distance*): It was me, Sir—*Gawd!* Ain't you ashamed o' yerself?

General laughter from all voices along corridor and on stage.

GUARD (*to unseen tower guard*): Jenkins! Go get those bastards!

Sound of a heavy stick banging on metal doors, fading into distance—then silence. GUARD *appears.*

ROCKY (*singing old hymn*):
Rock of ages, cleft for me-ee
Let me hide meself in thee-hee—

GUARD (*entering cell*): That's just lovely—Tibber! I can hardly wait to hear the rest at the Christmas concert.

ROCKY: Thanks, Cap! Bring the wife and kids. They deserve a treat for living with you all year.

GUARD: I'd as soon see them into a monkey cage at the zoo.

ROCKY: Fine sense of loyalty to your students, professor! Tch-tch . . . You hurt my feelin's.

QUEENIE: How do you think the monkeys must feel? Speakin' of monkeys, where in hell's the Mona Lisa?

GUARD: I took it over to the library. It's tryin' to find some book it needs for a number in the Christmas concert.

QUEENIE: I don't need no book for my act! What's she gonna do . . . read "Alice in Wonderland"?

GUARD: I believe it's hunting on the Shakespeare shelf.

QUEENIE: Oh no, who does she think she is . . . Bette Davis?

GUARD: As long as it doesn't ask me to play Romeo, I couldn't care less.

QUEENIE: "But soft, what balcony from yonder Juliet breaks . . ."

SMITTY: Mona shouldn't try to do Shakespeare here. They'd probably laugh, and . . .

QUEENIE: And what? Don't you think we could use a good laugh around this dump? Let her do it if she's fool enough. She'd be worse tryin' to do my act.

SMITTY: But they might hurt her feelings . . .

QUEENIE: Yeah? Maybe *you* should play Romeo. What do you think, Captain?

GUARD: I suppose a little Shakespeare's all right. We've never had the classics before. Maybe it'll start a whole new trend in Christmas concerts.

QUEENIE: Well I'll stick to song and dance and a few bumps and grinds.

SMITTY (*thinking aloud*): But why?

QUEENIE: Why bumps and grinds?

SMITTY: Huh? No . . . no, I was thinking of something else.

GUARD: Come on, Tibber . . . on your feet! They want you in the big office.

ROCKY: What in hell for?

GUARD: Well, I'm reasonably sure it's not to give you the Nobel Peace Prize.

ROCKY: I ain't done nothin'.

GUARD: I wouldn't know. I got a few dozen other characters to watch besides you. Make it fast. I've got to bring the Shakespearean actress back before lights out.

ROCKY: Crap! Roll me some smokes for later, Smitty!

SMITTY: Yeah! I'll try to keep busy so I don't miss you.

ROCKY *and* GUARD *exit.*

QUEENIE (*sings first three lines of* "*I'll See You Again*" *after them*): You don't smoke, an' you spend half your time rollin' smokes for that haywire goon. What's the matter with you?

SMITTY (*dryly*): We're "buddies."

QUEENIE: I'd like to know how he got you to make a mistake like that! I had an idea when I first saw you that you're the kind of guy who'd like to be on top.

SMITTY: Of what?

QUEENIE: Of everything. You're no lolliflier—you don't have to play it the way I do. Whatever you're gonna be here . . . you gotta be it in a big way. My way, I'm happy. The hippos know I'm a mean bitch, so I got no questions to answer. But I'm nobody's punk, and you shouldn't be either.

SMITTY: So what am I supposed to do . . . let you pick me

an old man? How the hell would that make any difference?

QUEENIE: You don't need a old man, you could be a hippo, if you play your cards right.

SMITTY: So deal me a hand, and see if it comes up a winner.

QUEENIE: Okay. Here's a straight. Rocky's nowhere near top dog in this joint . . . just a hard crap disturber who gets a wide berth from everybody. He ain't in at all, and as long as you're with him, you ain't either. If you get out from under Rocky, and I spread the news you're boss in this block, they'll listen.

SMITTY: So how do I do it? Give him to some sucker for Christmas?

QUEENIE: Who'd take him as a gift? You could wrap him up, just the same.

SMITTY: I'm tempted. What would I use, crap paper?

QUEENIE: You ain't scared of Rocky?

SMITTY: Hell no! I just figured he helped to keep me out of the storeroom. He said if I was asked to that party, I wouldn't be a guest, and I didn't like the idea of providing entertainment for anybody's wolf pack.

QUEENIE: So that's how he caught you . . . the cagey bastard.

SMITTY: You going to sound off about that?

QUEENIE: Not on your life! It wouldn't do me any good to broadcast how Rocky conned you into his nest. When I tipped you off to the storeroom gang splash, it was a cue to get next to the politicians who can do you some good. You shouldn't have give in so soon, or so easy.

SMITTY: Were you here?

QUEENIE: No, damn it!

SMITTY: Well, let me tell you, it wasn't so easy.

QUEENIE: Yeah? Can you go?

SMITTY: You think I didn't fight?

QUEENIE: So how come Rocky won?

SMITTY: With his mouth! Every time he said storeroom, I remembered about Mona, and my fists melted like candy floss.

QUEENIE (*excited*): You takin' a shower tonight?

SMITTY: I don't know. I try to make them few and far between. If I had a choice, I'd be dirty as a craphouse rat before taking a shower with Rocky.

QUEENIE: Take one tonight, and I'll give six. One thing about Rocky, he don't squeal.

SMITTY: What did you say?

QUEENIE: I'll . . . give . . . *six!*

SMITTY: Well! How do you think I should play it?

QUEENIE: You wanta be on top, don't ya? I ain't interested in no stars can't live up to their billing. If I put it out that you're tellin' Rocky an' me what to do, I gotta believe half of it.

SMITTY: I begin to read you. You want me to punch his head in. Right?

QUEENIE: Have you got what it takes?

SMITTY: All stored up!

QUEENIE: Then let it go.

SMITTY: In the crapper?

QUEENIE: I'll give you six in case Holy Face is hangin' around, but try and make it fast. Turn on a coupla showers to cover the slammin'.

SMITTY: You're on. Oh! Oh! Hold it a minute! What about after?

QUEENIE: What about it?

SMITTY: What will I owe you? You're not doing this out of sweet charity.

QUEENIE: Am I so hard to be nice to?

SMITTY: That depends . . .

QUEENIE: I mean . . . when you want and how you want— I'm nobody's old man, if you know what I mean.

SMITTY: It'd be a change, anyway.

QUEENIE: Whatever you want. You'll be top dog in this corner.

SMITTY: Six!

Sound of key in corridor door . . . enter GUARD *and* ROCKY.

GUARD: Slipped out of that one like a snake, didn't you, Tibber?

ROCKY: Sure! I don't let no finks hang me on the hook.

GUARD: You'll get caught one day, and when you do, I want to be there.

ROCKY: And here I thought you was my true friend.

GUARD: You make no friends, Tibber!

ROCKY: I got Smitty. I tell him everything . . . but everything, screw.

GUARD: That's his business.

ROCKY: Now, don't ya wish ya hadn't slapped me across the mouth three years ago, Mr. Screw?

GUARD: If I had to worry about every mouth I slapped around here, I'd be better off working as a wet nurse.

ROCKY: Well, maybe ya slug so many, ya forgot, but I ain't. It was my first day in the joint, an' I didn't call you "sir."

GUARD: You always were a nervy little brat.

ROCKY: So ya said, an' ya smashed me across the jaw wit' both sides o' yer big mitt, an' when I says, "Ain't y'afraid I'll tell the Warden?" ya says, why should ya be; twenty years ago ya smacked me father in the mouth, an' he was a thief an' a pimp just like me. Ain't that so, Hack?

GUARD: Yeah, that's it all right.

ROCKY: So-o, how's it feel t' have yer own arse roastin' over the pit—an' fer a little fifty-buck boo-boo?

GUARD: You bastard! (*Exits.*)

ROCKY: Oh, how sweet it is. (*Laughing.*) See how I shake 'em up, Smitty old kid? (*Stretches out on his bed.*) Say, where's my weeds, pal?

SMITTY: Roll your own—pal.

ROCKY *rolls a cigarette without taking his eyes from Smitty's face.*

ROCKY: Gimme a light, kid!

SMITTY (*tossing a lighter to* ROCKY): Light on your ass!

ROCKY (*carefully*): You two take a shower while The Rock was out on business?

QUEENIE (*coyly*): I should be so lucky.

ROCKY: Smitty, come here. I'm gonna tell you what happens to jokers what try to give Rocky the dirty end.

SMITTY: I can hear you.

ROCKY: That phony Wop, Catsolini, finked to a shop screw on me, an' now he's all wrapped up in the General's office . . . wishin' he'd kept his hole closed.

QUEENIE: I thought good old Catso was your machine-shop buddy.

ROCKY: Think again. He mouthed off to the machine-shop screw I lifted his lousy firebox, so they hauled me up to the General, give me a quick frisk, an' when they couldn't find nothin', put the pressure on me. I took it good for you, Smitty.

SMITTY: For me?

ROCKY: Sure! Where d'ya think you got your screwin' firebox—from Ronson's?

SMITTY: But I didn't want the bloody lighter. All I used it for was to light your crappin' smokes when you ask me to come on like your butler.

ROCKY: Alla same, I took it good so's they wouldn't put you on the spot, kid.

QUEENIE: My hero! They make medals for people like you and Saint Joan.

ROCKY: Can it! One thing about it, old Catso's headed for the tower as sure as Christ made little apples an' his mother's ass. His Wop temper got riled up when the screws started shovin' him, and he gave old Sad-Ass Shriker a punch in the mouth. He sure picked the wrong target. Shriker's had a rod-on for that Wop a mile long. Shriker don't like no sissies, micks, Wops, or Kikes, an' when he gets ahold of one, he's just gotta get 'em into the butcher shop so he can have his jollies.

QUEENIE: That's Mona's dearest boy friend . . . the one who slapped her little keester for her. I think she still dreams about him.

SMITTY: That's not funny, Queenie.

QUEENIE: Who says so? It gives me a laugh.

ROCKY: Six!

Sound of key in the door. Enter GUARD *and* MONA.

GUARD: Make way for the great Sarah Bernhardt . . . or is it Heartburn? (*Exits.*)

QUEENIE: Don't stand up; she's just passing through. No autographs, no interviews, no pictures, and please desist from climbing up on her balcony. Cripes! Look at the expression. She's takin' this tragic stuff serious. Pardon me, madam . . . do we perchance breathe the same air?

SMITTY: Leave her alone, Queenie. You look upset, Mona, what's eating you?

MONA (*trembling*): I . . . I saw something awful as I passed the hospital door.

QUEENIE: Don't tell me one of the boys was havin' a baby?

MONA: Tony . . .

QUEENIE (*quickly interested*): Catsolino?

MONA: Yes, he . . .

ROCKY: Cripes! Those screws musta really marked him up. That circus troupe he calls his family'll be cut off from Sunday visits while old Catso's walkin' around lookin' like a road map.

MONA: It wasn't just that.

SMITTY: What then, for God's sake?

MONA: The doctor was holding a stethoscope to his heart.

ROCKY: Maybe they wanted t' see if Wops has got one.

QUEENIE: I know what she means, an' so do you, rat. Some buddy you are to let him get it. See where Rocky takes his pals, Smitty?

SMITTY: What? Let me in on it.

QUEENIE: You wouldn't know of course. The butcher always tests your heart before he lets 'em cut you up in the kitchen.

SMITTY: What are you blowing about?

QUEENIE: There's a little room off the kitchen where they keep a machine an' a coupla long pieces of cowhide

. . . only that torture chamber ain't for the dumb animals.

SMITTY: They're not going to . . .

QUEENIE: You're goddam right they are. You don't slug a screw in the chops an' get off light. Catso's going to get the cat-o'-nine-tails.

SMITTY: God help him.

QUEENIE: Shall we pray?

ROCKY: The only time you get on your knees, bitch, it ain't to pray.

SMITTY: Over a lousy little firebox . . .

QUEENIE: Ease off Smitty. It ain't your beef.

SMITTY: The lighter was lifted for me.

ROCKY: That ain't what he's gettin' a ass-beat for. I got no sympathy for a bloody fink. All squealers oughta be shot.

SMITTY: Because of me . . .

ROCKY: You're buggy . . .

SMITTY (*to* MONA): What are you doing that for?

> MONA *is standing close to the upstage bars at the extreme end of wall, near the exit hall, poised in a position of straining to hear some sound from a great distance away. He seems completely occupied with the effort, unaware of the others in the room.*

QUEENIE: She's listening for the screams. Sometimes the screws leave the kitchen door open, an' you can just hear from that corner. Once I even heard the bloody slaps of the belt. Musta been old Shriker swingin'.

MONA: Oh-h-h . . . (*Does not seem to hear or see* SMITTY.)

QUEENIE: Oh, let her get 'er kicks. I think she's a goddam masochist.

SMITTY *crosses to pull* MONA *from bars almost brutally, but the boy does not seem to care; he only covers his ears with both hands, as though to shut out some sound.*

SMITTY (*voice shaking*): What do you want to do that for? You trying to bug me? Make me feel guilty?

MONA (*dazed*): I'm sorry . . . I'm sorry. (*Sits in trance on his bed.*)

ROCKY: I'm sick of this crap. Come on, Smitty, let's take a shower. For some reason I feel real good tonight.

SMITTY: Glad to hear it!

ROCKY: Jesus! Don't tell me you're actual gettin' co-operative?

SMITTY: I am . . . tonight.

ROCKY: We-ll, it's about time! Give us six, Mona, if you can come outa that stupor.

QUEENIE: Don't bug her! I'll give ya six tonight.

ROCKY: When did you get so friendly? I had the impression you didn't exactly like us leavin' you alone, Mother dear.

QUEENIE (*sweetly*): Tonight I like it. I'll baby-sit.

ROCKY: I smell a sardine, or two.

QUEENIE: What are ya worried about, Rocky? You must have a guilty conscience!

ROCKY: I got no conscience, an' no fat fruit worries me either. Come on, buddy boy.

SMITTY: You can call me Smith.

ROCKY: I don't care what I call ya as long as y' do like you're told. Now move your ass.

SMITTY *walks into the shower room.* ROCKY *turns a questioning look on* QUEENIE *who smiles in reply like the Cheshire cat.* ROCKY *goes out to shower room and* QUEENIE *crosses to stand near door to corridor, without looking toward shower-room door.*

MONA (*starting*): Something's wrong in there. What's that?

QUEENIE: Mind your screwin' business.

MONA: But Smitty . . .

QUEENIE: Can take care of himself. He's my boy now, and don't you forget it.

MONA: But Rocky . . .

QUEENIE: Is getting a lesson he's needed for a long time.

MONA: How do you . . . ?

QUEENIE: Because I can pick 'em real good, honey. I know a born hippo when I see one. I ain't spent time around these joints since I was fourteen for nothing. Smitty's got everythin' it takes to run his own show, but he needs me t' help him. I'm big-hearted that way.

MONA: There's no sound now . . .

QUEENIE: I said to make it fast. You give me six. I'm gonna check the damage. (QUEENIE *goes to shower room, returning almost at once.*) You still got that alcohol an' bandages I give you t' hide under your mattress?

MONA: You planned this—to get Smitty.

QUEENIE: Right where I can see him—like I got all the other suckers on this street.

MONA: He could have been caught—or killed. You're not even on his side.

QUEENIE: If he's got a side! Shut your nellie jaw, before I blind you, bitch—an' get me that goddam medicine bag.

MONA: Yes—I'll get it.(*He does so.*)

QUEENIE: An' get ready to bow low, Miss Shakespeare. This block had a good queen; all it needed was a king. (*Exits triumphantly, leaving* MONA *looking lost and alone.*)

Curtain

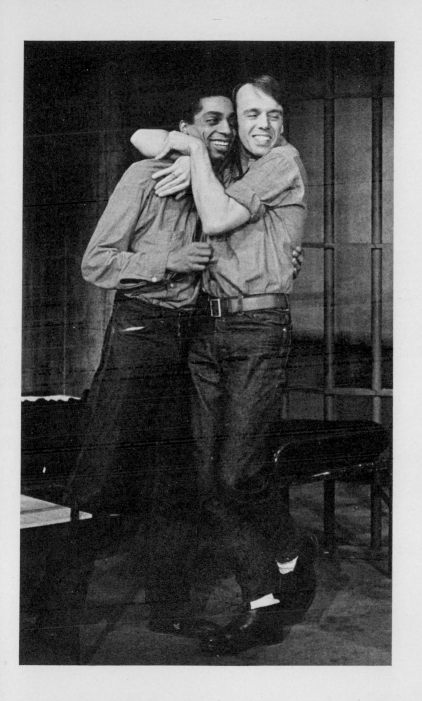

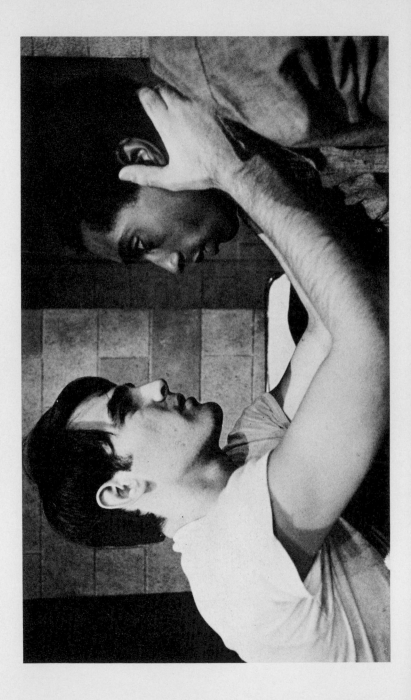

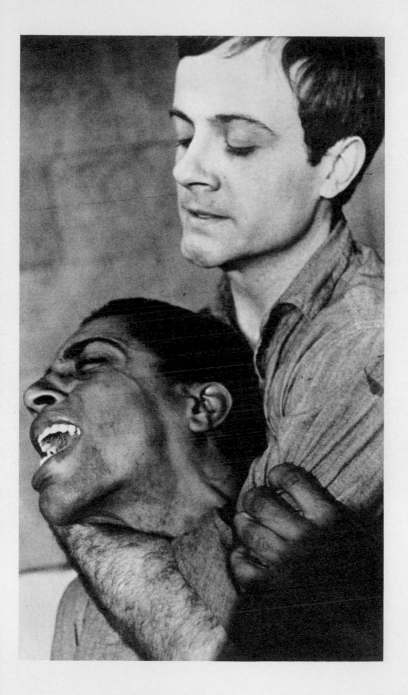

Photos by Henry Grossman

ACT TWO

Christmas Eve.

At one end of dormitory, ROCKY *lies smoking, on his bed: at the other end,* SMITTY *is propped up on his, with a book, reading: the* GUARD, *Holy Face, sits on a high stool, upstage, and a portable record player is going, the music filling the dormitory with something of a night-club atmosphere.*

ROCKY: Crap, Captain! The Christmas stunt is lousy enough, without havin' t' watch stinkin' rehearsals.

GUARD: We could always arrange to reserve you a private room, Mr. Tibber. There's a vacancy right now in Gunsel's Alley . . .

ROCKY: Screw off!

GUARD: If you think this is any treat for me, guess again. I got a television when I want to be entertained. The tumblers and acrobats and what-have-you are using up the stage and gym floor, so the leading ladies will just have to practice here at home, with the family. You are what might be described as a captive audience. (*Walking toward shower-room door.*) Move it, girls . . . you're on! These critics of yours will be asleep before you get into those costumes.

QUEENIE (*calling from shower room*): Thank you, Mr. Sullivan. A little cruisin' music, please, while I remove my jock. I'll take it from the top . . . as we used to say at the Casino.

The GUARD *crosses to reset the record, and* QUEENIE *enters, looking like a combination of Gorgeous George, Sophie Tucker and Mae West. He wears a platinum-blond wig, spangled sequin dress, long black gloves, large rhinestone jewelry on ears, neck and wrists, heavy make-up and is carrying a large feather fan. There is no self-consciousness or lack of confidence: movements are large, controlled, voluptuous and sure. He throws open the fan, as* ROCKY, SMITTY *and the* GUARD *watch, bending his knees in a slow dip, so the tight gown pulls across his heavy, rounded body, giving the look of an overweight strip teaser beginning the act; slowly he undulates the hips forward and upward in a series of professionally controlled bumps and grinds, the meat and muscle of burlesque dancing. As the record plays the opening to a song, an old night-club favorite,* QUEENIE *prepares the way with these bold, sex-conscious movements.*

SMITTY: Holy mother of . . . you look sexy as hell. Look what we had here, and didn't know it.

QUEENIE: It's all your, honey—every precious pound. (*Picks up the melody from the recording, to sing a parody of "A Good Man Is Hard to Find."*)

Here is a story, without morals
An' all you fags better pay some mind
'Cause if ya find a man worth keepin'
Be satisfied—an' treat him kind.

A hard man is good to find
I always get the other kind
Just when I think that he's my pal
I turn around an' find him actin' like somebody's gal
And then I rave; I even crave

To see him lyin' dead in his grave.
So if your hippo's nice
Take my advice
Hug him in the shower, kiss him every night
Give him plenty oompah, treat him right
'Cause a hard man nowadays is good to find.

There is spontaneous applause, from even ROCKY *and the* GUARD, *for there is an all-embracing extrovert quality to Queenie's performance that is somehow contagious, partly because of a warmth generated by a feeling that* QUEENIE *seems completely happy with himself and his surroundings.*

ROCKY: Come on, Queenie . . . give us another one . . . real lowdown and dirty.

SMITTY: Yeah, Queenie . . . sing it for Daddy, and don't forget I like the wiggle accompaniment.

QUEENIE (*like a famous star*): Sorry, boys . . . that's gotta wait for the show. Get your tickets early, before the front seats are sold out. I wouldn't wantya t' miss anything headed your way.

SMITTY: Throw it here, kid; I don't need a catcher's mitt.

ROCKY: Turn that stuff on again, Queenie; I might get in the mood.

QUEENIE: Put your gloves on, boys. We ain't got that much time before the show starts, an' this is more or less a costume an' make-up rehearsal. We got our numbers down already, but they didn't get these Christmas decorations in till today. Ain't this gown a flip?

SMITTY: Fits like a second skin. What did you do . . . grow into it?

QUEENIE: I hadda get Mona to shove me with a shoehorn.

SMITTY: What you hiding under there?

QUEENIE: Nothing, baby—but your Christmas box.

ROCKY: I'll look after the diamonds for ya.

QUEENIE: They musta took a chandelier apart to get all this glass. Feels good, but you couldn't hock it for a plate o' beans.

ROCKY: Looks like they shot a ostrich for ya, too.

QUEENIE (*waving the fan*): I hope it ain't moulting season in Africa.

SMITTY: You sprung those curls awful fast.

QUEENIE: My teeth an' my ass are my own, Honey!

GUARD (*caught in the mood*): If my wife could see me now, she'd start divorce proceedings.

QUEENIE: Never mind, baby; think of the beautiful music you an' me could make while she's in Mexico.

ROCKY: As long as you're spreadin' it around, Queenie . . . my pad's over here. Holy Face ain't got anythin' I can't better.

QUEENIE (*enjoying every moment*): What am I bid? Line up the Cadillacs on stage left an' the mink coats on the right. What's your offer, Smitty?

SMITTY: All I got is this book on auto mechanics.

QUEENIE (*with a wink*): Oh, that ain't all you got, Honey.

SMITTY (*laughing*): You've been peeking again.

ROCKY: Turn on the walkin' music, Queenie, an' give us the strip you did at the last Christmas concert.

QUEENIE: Are you kidding? I did a week in the tower for that surprise performance. I could hear the boys still whistlin', when they turned the key on your mother. Oh well, the bread an' water was good for my figure. I started the New Year lookin' like a cover off Vogue!

GUARD: No more surprises like that one, Queenie, or your concert days will be over. The conveners of this one had a hell of a time getting the General to trust you again.

QUEENIE: Oh, I told them how to fix that up.

GUARD: That's news to me. What did you do?

QUEENIE: I promised the General a little bit.

> ROCKY, SMITTY *and the* GUARD *laugh uproariously. At this moment,* MONA *enters, wearing a makeshift costume for Portia's court scene in* The Merchant of Venice. *It is a converted red velvet curtain and becomes him somewhat, but contrast between the graceful, almost classic costume and Queenie's glittering ensemble seems incongruous.*

ROCKY: Flyin' crap! What's that supposed to be? Your bathrobe an' nightcap? What're ya gonna do . . . "The Night Before Christmas"?

QUEENIE (*in impresario fashion*): Ladies and gentlemen, I want you all to meet Tillie—The Birdwoman, God's gift to the Tree People.

> ROCKY, SMITTY *and* GUARD *howl at the announcement,*

but MONA *remains as enigmatic in expression as the painting he is named for.*

What kinda music do you want, Tillie . . . a slow waltz or a minuet? You'll never get those window drapes off the ground.

MONA: I won't need music.

QUEENIE: Well, you need something. (*Proffering the fan.*) How about these feathers? If you wave 'em hard enough, they might lift you up on your toes; you could call it "The Dying Duck" ballet.

ROCKY: Maybe she oughta have a window to hang herself in.

QUEENIE: You better not do a strip, 'cause you'd hafta have red flannel underwear to go with that smock.

MONA: It's from "The Merchant of Venice."

QUEENIE: Well, I'd take it back to him, dearie; you got gypped, whatever you paid.

MONA: This costume is for the courtroom scene . . .

QUEENIE: Oh, I get it. You're gonna play a judge. That should go over big in this joint.

MONA: It's Portia . . .

QUEENIE: It's poor something.

SMITTY (*sober and fierce suddenly*): Cut it, Queenie!

QUEENIE: What's biting your backside, big boy? She oughta be able to take a little fun.

SMITTY: You go past the point where it's funny.

QUEENIE: When I want you to tell me what to laugh at, I'll write you a certificate of authority.

GUARD (*standing*): Okay, children . . . cool it! Or we cut the run-through right here.

QUEENIE: Let's have Miss Shakespeare's number. I'm sure Rocky and the other boys will just love it, especially the ones who write poems on the wall of the crapper.

SMITTY: I know the scene, Mona; we took it in high-school English. It's where Portia goes to court for her boyfriend. Isn't that the part?

MONA (*attention on* SMITTY *only*): Yes . . . it is the plea she makes in the name of human charity and . . .

SMITTY (*gently*): Mercy?

MONA: Yes.

SMITTY: I'd like to hear it again. Will you say it for me?

QUEENIE: Oh mercy my me!

The others move into the background, sitting on beds, the GUARD *returns to his stool. They watch, as though at some amusing spectacle, where one should not laugh, but cannot resist.* QUEENIE *pokes* ROCKY *in the ribs with his elbow. Then opens the fan over his face, holding it as a shield.* ROCKY *casually lights a cigarette and the* GUARD *yawns with indifference. Only* SMITTY *moves to hear* MONA, *looking into the serious, sad face.*

MONA *begins very hesitantly, stuttering (with comic pathos and badly spoken)—as others giggle and roll eyes, etc.*

QUEENIE *and* ROCKY *interrupt Mona's speech through-out.*

MONA:
The quality of mercy is not strained,
It droppeth, as the gentle rain from heaven
Upon the place beneath: it is twice blessed;
It blesseth him that gives, and him that takes:
'Tis mightiest in the mightiest; it becomes
The throned monarch better than his crown;
His sceptre shows the force of temporal power
The attribute to awe and majesty,
Wherein doth sit the dread and fear of kings;
But mercy is above this sceptred sway,
It is enthroned in the hearts of kings,
It is an attribute of God himself;
And earthly power doth then show likest God's,
When mercy seasons justice.

QUEENIE (*to* SMITTY, *standing*): Down in front.

SMITTY *sits and* MONA *strives to continue.*

(*With finality:*)
Thank you!

MONA *continues.*

ROCKY: Take it off.

QUEENIE: Put it on.

ROCKY: Ya dropped yer lunch.

QUEENIE: Encore!

ROCKY: Turn off the lights.

QUEENIE: Gee, you're pretty, lady!

ROCKY: Pretty ugly.

QUEENIE: Would you mind terribly—coming out of a cake?

MONA *falters and seems unable to continue.*

Oh, she doesn't know it by heart.

SMITTY (*turning to the* GUARD): Will you make them shut up?

GUARD: Okay. Good enough! The guys are waitin' and they won't know them words any better 'n you do. Let's go, Christmas dolls! Come on, Shirley Dimples—and you too, Raggedy Ann!

QUEENIE (*grabbing* MONA *away from* SMITTY): Laws has muhcy, Miss Melanie—de Yankees is hyeah. Ain' you skeered dey gonna find yoah sissy brudder in dat closet? (*Propelling* MONA *toward corridor and concert.*) Run foh yoah life; all Atlanta am on fiyah!

They exit.

GUARD (*to* ROCKY *and* SMITTY): You bums get busy with a boot brush, and button up those shirt fronts. The General's wife and the Salvation Army are out there tonight. (*He exits.*)

ROCKY (*shouting after him*): Yeah! I'll wear me best tie— de one wit' de stripes. Queenie's browned off with you, Smitty.

SMITTY: Who gives a screw?

ROCKY: Mona . . . maybe?

SMITTY: How come Mona bothers you so much? You got a rod-on for her?

ROCKY: I got something I'd like t' give all fruits, but it ain't what they're lookin' for.

SMITTY: Seems to me that Mona doesn't know you're alive.

ROCKY: Oh, the Mona knows I'm here all right, only it's too lily-livered to look.

SMITTY: For a joker who claims he doesn't go in that direction, it looks to me like you ride the train awful hard.

ROCKY: You tryin' t' prove somethin', wise guy?

SMITTY: I don't have to. You prove the point every time you open your trap . . . it snaps shut on what you are.

ROCKY: Don't ever get the idea I'm a pansy, punker!

SMITTY: Watch your words there, Rocky. I'm nobody's punker these days, or have you forgotten what the floor of the crapper smells like . . . up close?

ROCKY: I ain't forgot.

SMITTY: Don't make me remind you too often.

ROCKY: Y' use your meat hooks pretty good, but that don't make you big time, Mister. Queenie tells me you're doin' a lousy little joy-ride rap. That's kid stuff.

SMITTY: It's big enough for me.

ROCKY: Ya didn't know yer ass from a hole in the ground before ya hit this joint here. It took me and Queenie t' smarten y' up.

SMITTY: I'm not interested in getting smart like you or Queenie. Did you get a chance to keep any of the stuff you got knocked off for? I guess not. And it must have taken a lot of Queenie's guts to smash a little old lady over the head for a closetful of diamonds and furs.

ROCKY: I'da got away clean if the lousy heap didn't run outa stinkin' gas, but Queenie screwed herself . . . she hadda play the actress before sluggin' some old bitch, by standin' in the hall singin' Happy Birthday to cover up the screams. Too bad the next-door neighbor knew it wasn't the old dame's birthday, and called the cops. Crap! I'da gave my right eye to 'a seen Queenie's face when they put the arm on her with that load of mink coats and diamonds. I'll bet she was plannin' to wear 'em, like Queen Elizabeth, on Halloween.

SMITTY: So today she's wearing a neckload of cheap glass and singing her songs to a gymnasium full of pickpockets and petty boosters.

ROCKY: Well, I ain't in that class. When my bit's up here, my real old man'll be outa Kingston, and me and him's gonna hit the big time together. I guess a pun . . . (*he thinks better of using the term*) . . . a joy-rider like you don't know who Tiger Tibber is.

SMITTY: Sure . . . I've read about your father . . . the high priest of pipe dreams.

ROCKY: But you wouldn't know what kinda cash a guy gets, dealin' out the junk.

SMITTY: Look Rocky, I don't give a crap what you and your old man do to get back here or someplace else. Queenie's always telling me what a big thing it is to pry open somebody's door or window, and you want to impress me by telling me your father peddles dope and your mother sells bingo to wine-hounds. Well, it cuts no ice with me. If I was to choose a racket it wouldn't be lousy drugs and cheap booze.

ROCKY: Well, ya better find somethin', buddy boy, 'cause y'ain't gonna be able t' git a decent job no more—maybe not even a half-assed one. Lookit Queenie! She wuz workin' the counter o' a Chinatown restaurant, after her first bit here. She wuzn't there two weeks when Seven-Foot Tiny o' the Morality Squad steps inta the kitchen t' scoff a free cuppa coffee. He catches sight o' sweet Queenie playin' tea maid t' all them tourists 'n' square Chinks, so sends down t' the cash register fer the manager. He asks him does he know he's got a queer an' a thief workin' fer 'im. Dear Queenie, who planned on gittin' fat that winter, wuz out in the alley wit' the rest o' the cats—before Big Tiny finishes his bummy cuppa coffee.

SMITTY: So? Queenie made a try, anyway. It was probably better than selling bingo to wine-hounds. You pick your form of animal life; I'll find mine.

ROCKY: You keep my old lady outa it. When she was a big-time bootlegger she use'ta eat little boys like you for breakfast.

SMITTY: I can believe it!

ROCKY: And she still rakes in more dough in a day than you seen in a year.

SMITTY: I hope she saves it to pay her fines. They must love her at City Hall.

ROCKY: Can it.

SMITTY: You started this bomb rolling, big mouth.

ROCKY: That's what I get for tryin' to level withya about Queenie! She's bugged by you playin' nursemaid to Mona.

SMITTY: I don't like to see somebody shoved around by a couple of yellow-bellied crapheads.

ROCKY: You tangled with Queenie yet?

SMITTY: I'm ready when it comes!

ROCKY: I got news for you. Queenie's in solid with the politicians. She keeps old Baldy fixed up with punkers, and he pays by takin' the jokers she fingers, and lockin' em up in Gunsel's Alley.

SMITTY: I'm worried sick; notice how my nails are chewed to the elbow.

ROCKY: You ain't done hard time till they make you sit it out in Gunsel's Alley. Y'eat, crap, wash, jerk an' flop . . . all in a lonely little six-by-six. It's real cozy if ya don't go haywire the first month. A couple goons smashed their own heads on the brick wall . . . wide open like eggs. They figgered they was better off in the hospital than locked alone in a cage, like a screwin' canary.

SMITTY: I'd sing all day long, if I thought I wouldn't have to look at your ugly map for the rest of my time.

ROCKY: Yeah? Well they don't let little Mona drop in for visits, y' know.

SMITTY: Let's take a shower, Rocky!

ROCKY: I'm nice and clean right now, thanks.

SMITTY: Well don't rub any more of your dirt on me, 'cause I'll get the urge to clean it off . . . on you. Dig me, punk?

GUARD (*entering with* MONA): Okay Hans and Fritz! Patch it up and come on to the Christmas concert. They've got a bag of candies and an orange waiting for you at the door.

SMITTY: Why aren't you backstage, Mona? It's about time to start.

MONA: They decided I shouldn't do any Shakespeare.

SMITTY: Who decided?

MONA: Mr. Benson said they would only laugh at me and make life more unpleasant afterwards.

SMITTY: Well come on and watch with me, then.

GUARD: No, leave it here! Whenever that one gets into an assembly, there's trouble. Last time it was at church-up . . . somebody split its pants down the back with a razor blade.

SMITTY: You wouldn't call that his fault.

GUARD: Look, Junior! If you had a bunch of hunters waving rifles around, you wouldn't throw a bird in the air, and expect nobody to shoot, would ya? It stays here.

SMITTY: This is Christmas!

GUARD: I don't care if it's the day of the Second Coming, the target stays here. Anyhow, it's got the whole corridor to roam around in tonight. The cell doors are all open, an' silly-bitch can go sniffin' around the empty beds for entertainment.

SMITTY: Isn't there a rule that says everybody attends the Christmas concert?

GUARD: You ask too many questions, Smith.

SMITTY: I thought you went by *all* the rules.

GUARD (*uneasy, as sometimes with Rocky's words*): Yeah! Come on, let's go.

SMITTY: I'll celebrate right here.

GUARD: Pick the kind of company you want, Smith, but take my advice . . . don't get caught. Come on, Tibber.

ROCKY: Let's move! The concert can't be as corny as this act. So long, sweethearts.

GUARD *and* ROCKY *exit.*

In the distance, Boys' voices can be heard singing a round of:

Row, row, row your boat,
Gently down the stream
Merrily, merrily, merrily, merrily,
Life is but a dream . . .

Sounds are from gathering in auditorium.

SMITTY: I hate that son of a bitch, and I'm soon going to show him how much. Then, he'll know the shower of knuckles I gave him was only a baptism.

MONA: Rocky can destroy himself soon enough.

SMITTY: He ought to be squashed—like a bedbug.

MONA: What would you expect of him? Do you know that his father . . .

SMITTY: Hell, yes! He takes great pride in his parents—the famous dope-peddler and the fabulous bootlegger. He sure rounds out that family circle.

MONA: Before he came here, this time, his mother was sent to jail. She's been convicted so many times, the court wouldn't accept another fine.

SMITTY: My heart bleeds for the dear, lost lady and her deprived offspring. Who'll make the pancakes now and run the still?

MONA: Rocky's sixteen-year-old brother took over the bootlegging and began, besides, to sell his teen-age girl friends to anybody who has five dollars.

SMITTY: Say! Outside, did you live near that slum?

MONA: No, I probably wouldn't have lived this long, or, at least, my nose would be a different shape.

SMITTY: How come you know so much about the rockhead?

MONA: I listen to him and read between the lines.

SMITTY: What a waste of time! That's their mess—not ours. I'm interested in you and me. You make excuses for them, but you keep your secrets, like Greta Garbo—under a hat.

MONA: You haven't said much about your life outside.

SMITTY: I'm forgetting, that's why—I'm going to spend the rest of my life forgetting my father. He put me here. To hell with him! Who put you in?

MONA: No one—really! It just—happened.

SMITTY: Happened? How can a thing like getting here just happen?

MONA: My life—like that from the start; I expect what comes.

SMITTY: That tells me a lot.

MONA: It's just that I can't . . .

SMITTY: So shove it, then!

MONA: A gang—of guys—in the neighborhood—that night —pushed me around. My payday—had it on me—they knew. Next thing—I'm on the ground—kicking me— kicking. I look up—all those legs, but there's a big cop. Thank God! Thank God! Bleeding—numb—on my feet at last! Then—he looked at me, and I saw his sympathy shift—to the gang. Forgot my money—excited; asked were they mixed up with me—sexually. Smitty?

SMITTY: Don't get off the damn pot! Crap it out!

MONA: A—a huddle—like a football game—formation; all came out, laid charges—said I made passes. Four gave witness in court. Only voice for me—my poor, shocked mother, and sitting out there, trying to smile at me—eyes dark, afraid—God help her—my young sister!

SMITTY: But you should have had a lawyer.

MONA: Oh, I had one—or did I? Yeah—too late, after he got his money—we saw he didn't care—to tarnish his reputation. No real defense. A deal. Magistrate's court is like trial in a police station—all pals, lawyers and cops together! Threw me on the mercy of the court. Oh, Christ—that judge, with his hurry-up face, heard the neat police evidence and my lawyer's silly, sugar-sweet plea. So halfhearted—I wanted to shout,

"Let me speak; leave me some damn dignity!" The fat, white-haired frown looked down at me—"Go to jail for six months!"—like I'd dirtied his hands, and that would wipe them clean. Six months! Six thousand would have sounded the same.

SMITTY: Well, things are going to be a lot different by next month. There's a brand new year on the way.

MONA: How—"different"?

SMITTY: I mean, you're not going to be pushed around by anybody—goons, like Rocky and Queenie. They taught me more than was good for them. I'm on my way to being a politician, and I don't plan to do anymore hard time because of anybody. We've had it rough lately, but I'm about to even the score.

MONA: I don't know how that can be done.

SMITTY: Hell, kid! What I'm saying is we're going to wear the best of everything—new shirts, fresh from the tailor shop, and lightweight boots. We'll get extra grub—candy and fresh fruit—everything good that's going around. What do you say to that?

MONA: What do you expect me to say—about those things?

SMITTY: Well, for cripe's sake you might say "thanks." I'll have to. Or, "I like you, Smitty," or even—you might—

MONA: What's happened to you, Smitty?

SMITTY: I discovered I'm human. You're not blind. Who's been acting like your old man lately?

MONA: I don't have any old man. I thought you understood that.

SMITTY: You only think you don't. Look, Jan, when I came to this joint, I didn't know up from down. I've made a few mistakes since the one that got me here, and that's the only one I'm not sorry for. I stole a car—to get my mother out of town, away from my drunken slob of a father. I had to—he had the keys. I was helping her to run away with Ben—Ben's a nice guy. They tried to get me out of this jackpot, together, but I slugged a cop when they were arresting me. My dear father got back at us all. He didn't have a good word for me in court. After all, he was the respectable married man, a substantial citizen with his own business—the hardhearted bastard! Hard is a good word for him. He likes hard women, hard liquor, and hard words. For all he wanted from my mother, he might as well have hired a housekeeper and visited a prostitute regularly. Screw him! What I'm saying is you've got to work at it to make things go your way.

MONA: I can see you're not going to park your keester in a corner. Your father and Queenie have taught you well.

SMITTY: And I'm sick of that fat whore treating me like a piece of her property. I'll pick my own bedmate from here in. I shouldn't have to give you all this jazz, you know what I need. Haven't you any feelings after all?

MONA: Yes—some, but not the kind you're getting at—at least, not with you.

SMITTY: What did you say?

MONA: I said—not with you, Smitty.

SMITTY: Saving yourself for those dirty bastards in the

gym? Is that what you enjoy—being forced into a corner?

MONA: It's better that way.

SMITTY: Better? Are you playing hard to get or something? Because, I know different; anybody who grabs you, gets you.

MONA: Slicings—patterns—blind and empty release; sure, I'll go on being a party to it.

SMITTY: Do you like that? I thought you liked me.

MONA: I do, Smitty—a great deal.

SMITTY: I knew you put up with what you got because you had no choice; that you really went for me. You showed it in a hundred ways, so now, while we're alone—a chance—

MONA: Just a minute! How do you feel with Queenie—afterward?

SMITTY: I could spit on her.

MONA: It would be the same with me; it's not in your nature.

SMITTY: I came to you.

MONA: No! Just circumstance! You're looking for a girl—not for me.

SMITTY: Do I smell or something? What's wrong with *my* body?

MONA: Nothing—it's very—Smitty, don't ask me to.

SMITTY: Should I ask you to do it with somebody else? Keep on being public property? I guess you like change—a different one every day, for variety. What do you do? Make comparison?

MONA: I—separate! Yes, that's right. I separate things in order to live with others and myself. What my body does and feels is one thing, and what I think and feel apart from that is something else.

SMITTY: You're crazy.

MONA: It's to the world I dream in you belong. It endures better. I won't let you move over, into the other, where I would become worthless to you—and myself. I have a right to save something.

SMITTY: I was afraid of everyone—everything—except you —until now. You're trying to shake me.

MONA: You're trying to kill me. You think I can be used just any old way—even by you.

SMITTY: To hell with me then!

MONA: No—listen! It's the sight of myself I can't stand— the way you throw it back.

SMITTY: Where do you get the goddam gall to tell me how I see you?

MONA: The right to say or be anything or everything or nothing to myself—and not a tame little fruit. Wasn't that it—soft, worshiping, harmless? Now you've flexed your muscles and found power, I'm an easy convenience. Not a Queenie! Oh no; I'd never turn on you. If I mattered, you'd be afraid of my feelings— not sure of them. You're offering me—indifference. Well, I don't want it.

SMITTY: Did you think I wanted your body? You make me sick. I wanted some kind of reaction to me, and only because I'm caught in this hellhole, you filthy fairy! You cocksucker!

MONA: You see? You see?

SMITTY (*runs to the bars*): Let me out of here! I'll go to the bloody concert—anywhere—where there's life—

He bangs wildly on bars with his fists. MONA *follows to stand behind* SMITTY, *puts out a hand gently, but not touching him, then with difficulty, punches him on the shoulder.* SMITTY *reacts violently, turning on* MONA.

MONA: No! Wait a minute! (*Goes to Smitty's bunk, picks up a book and holds it out.*) Look—listen—you read it.

SMITTY *goes slowly to sit beside* MONA *and begins to read, clumsily, haltingly. They laugh, embarrassed, and continue to read until they are in a slight hysteria of laughter that causes them to break up and fall against each other.*

When in disgrace with fortune and men's eyes
I, all alone, beweep my outcast state,
And trouble deaf heaven with my bootless cries,
And look upon myself, and curse my fate,
Wishing me like to one more rich in hope,
Featur'd like him, like him with friends possess'd,
Desiring this man's art, and that man's scope,
With what I most enjoy, contented least;
Yet in these thoughts myself almost despising,
Haply I think on thee, and then my soul
(Like to the lark at break of day arising,

From sullen earth) sings hymns at heaven's gate;
For thy sweet love remembered such wealth brings,
That then I scorn to share my state with kings.

SMITTY *and* MONA *are laughing, heads close together,
when* QUEENIE *and* ROCKY *enter.*

QUEENIE: I'll give the bitch a bluebird! (*Smashes his fist
into Mona's cheek.*)

ROCKY: Give it to the dirty little fruit.

SMITTY (*who has leaped up, fists ready to swing. He
punches* QUEENIE *on the jaw*): Screw off, bastard!

QUEENIE (*backing away, but preparing to fight*): I'll take
the punk, Rocky. Put your boots to the bitch.

SMITTY *turns to take* ROCKY, *and* QUEENIE *uses the
advantage to put a wrestling hold on* SMITTY, *pinning
his arms behind his back.*

I got him. Go, Rocky! Go!

ROCKY (*shaking* MONA *as though he were a rag doll*): I'm
gonna smash your face, fairy.

He throws MONA *to the floor, raising his foot to kick,
but* SMITTY *breaks from* QUEENIE, *hurling the heavy
blond to the floor, and kicks* ROCKY *in the groin.* ROCKY
screams, doubling over with pain. SMITTY *then goes
after* QUEENIE *just as the* GUARD *comes in, gun drawn.*

GUARD: To the wall fast, or I cut your feet off.

All except MONA, *who lies on the floor, move toward
the wall.*

Raise those mitts, children!

The three raise hands.

Okay, crap-disturbers, what's the score here?

QUEENIE
ROCKY   (*together*)· That dirty little bitch . . . The
SMITTY   goddam fruit . . . These filthy bastards . . .

GUARD: Cut it! One at a time! (*To* QUEENIE:) You, Goldilocks, what's your story?

QUEENIE: When me an' Rocky come in from the concert, that lolliflier on the floor was tryin' to make the kid here. (*Wide-eyed.*) We done it for his own good, Cap!

GUARD: Yeah! I can just imagine your motives. (*To* ROCKY:) Okay, you now, Terrible Tibber! Let's hear your phony. Who were you saving?

ROCKY: Queenie give it to you straight, Cap; an' I'm stickin' with that story. The fruit was gropin' pretty good when we made the scene. We don't want that kinda stuff in here. You know how it is. Just turn your back an' that little queer's reachin' . . .

GUARD: Okay, turn it off, Tibber! Next thing you'll be telling me you want to go to church next Sunday to pray. (*To* SMITTY:) All right, Romeo! Let's have your version of the balcony scene.

SMITTY: My name is Smith.

GUARD: Well, well! May I call you Mister Smith? Names don't mean a damned thing in here, sonny. Actions mean everything. Did that thing on the floor make a pass at you?

SMITTY: Nobody made a pass.

GUARD: Oh, now, this isn't your mother or a judge you're talking to, Smarty Smith. We know by now a pass was made. I'm not asking you if you liked it. I want to know who made the pass.

SMITTY: Nobody made any pass at anybody.

GUARD: Real stubborn, aren't you?

SMITTY: You asked me. I can't help it that you don't believe me. We were talking when these haywire goons hit the block. They started the hey rube and I took over, since they seemed to want to play.

GUARD: You're not only getting too smart, Smith, you're becoming arrogant as well. Where do you think this attitude's going to lead you?

SMITTY: Into the office, where I can put an end to this crap.

GUARD: You're right . . . the General's office, where you'll need some much smarter answers.

SMITTY: I've got them.

GUARD: Your answers aren't worth much when you get hauled up on the big guy's carpet, kid.

SMITTY: Says you! Don't you think they might be worth about . . . fifty bucks?

The GUARD *is stunned into silence. He steals a quick accusing look at* ROCKY, *who averts his eyes carefully.*

GUARD (*shakily*): I don't think you know what you're talking about. What is this . . . some kind of bluff?

SMITTY: I don't say anything I can't back up with facts . . . like names, dates and letters. Dig me, screw?

GUARD (*enraged but cornered*): You crapping fink! Learned

it all, haven't you? Found a way to save your precious little hide? (*To* ROCKY:) I ought to shoot you a second mouth, Tibber.

ROCKY *just grins in reply, now enjoying the Guard's discomfiture.*

There's one hide's not going to get off so easy. (GUARD *pushes* MONA *with his foot.*) Up off your ass, you little pansy! You know what you got the last time this happened, don't you? (*He pushes* MONA *ahead of him, toward the corridor door.*) You can bend over all you want, in the kitchen.

MONA (*realizing*): No! Oh, no, no, no, no . . . (*Protest mounts to screams off-stage.*)

SMITTY (*running to the bars*): Stop it! Stop it! I did it! I made the pass. (*Shouting after them.*) Do you hear? I made the pass . . . I made the . . .

QUEENIE *and* ROCKY *begin to laugh in derision.*

(*Turning vicious.*) Shut up you yellow bastards! I'll wipe the floor with your rotten guts. One more laugh out of your ugly kissers and I'll spray teeth from here to hell.

QUEENIE: We didn't mean anything, Smitty. What are you so hot about? That little . . .

SMITTY: Shut your filthy hole, you fat whore!

ROCKY: Jeez, Smitty; that thing ain't worth . . .

SMITTY: Listen to me, Rock-ass! Before I leave this stinking joint I'm going to demolish your mug so bad that no fruit will ever look at you again . . . let alone a woman. When will depend on you. Ask for it once and you've

got it. This is my show from now on. I got that lousy
screw over a barrel, and I'm going to keep him there.
Also, Baldy's making me a politician . . . a wheel in
the office. You see, Queenie, I wasn't hustling my
little ass in the park at thirteen for peanuts. I went
to school; I got typing and bookkeeping, so Baldy's
put me where I can make things move my way. If
you'd learned to write, maybe you'd be better off . . .
but you'll swallow chicken crap when I make up the
menu. And you, monkey; would you like to be my
punchin' bag around here or should I ship you into
Gunsel's Alley for safekeeping? Choose fast!

ROCKY: I . . . I'll take it off you.

SMITTY: Okay. You'll volunteer to be my sparring partner
in the gym every time I want to box somebody, and,
sweetie, I'm gonna knock you senseless. Now get into
that goddam crapper and stick your heads into a
coupla bowls, till I yell for you to come out. That'll
be after lights out, 'cause I don't want to see your
ugly maps again today.

ROCKY *and* QUEENIE *look at each other, dazed.*

You know who Baldy is? You know what he can do?
Well, I'm his boy now.

QUEENIE: Ain't it the bitter truth? (*Pulls* ROCKY *away.*)
Come on, Snake-Eyes; we rolled too low in the game
—this time around.

SMITTY: So move, goddam it! (*A step toward them.*)

*In their haste to get out, the two bump into each
other, ridiculous and clumsy in their new roles.*
SMITTY *laughs loudly, revealing a cruelty that fills the*

room with its sound. Suddenly his head turns in another direction as though just recalling something. He steals a quick look toward the shower room, then stealthily and lithely as a cat, he moves to the corner of the dorm where MONA *had listened to the sound of Catsolino's beating. From an attitude of strained listening,* SMITTY *suddenly contorts in pain as* MONA *had done before, but there is no sound from his distorted mouth. He seems to be whipped by unseen strokes of a lash, until he is spread-eagled across the upstage bars. When it seems he can bear no more he covers his ears with both hands, stumbling blindly downstage. Standing thus, head and shoulders down, he rises slowly out of the hunched position to full height, hands lowering. His face now seems to be carved of stone, the mouth narrow, cruel and grim, the eyes corresponding slits of hatred. He speaks in a hoarse, ugly whisper.*

I'm going to pay them back.

He then walks, almost casually, down to Rocky's bunk where cigarettes, which we have not seen him use before, and a lighter, lie on the side table. He picks up a cigarette, lights it, then stretches out on Rocky's bed, torso upright against the back of it. Looking coolly out to the audience with a slight, twisted smile that is somehow cold, sadistic and menacing, he speaks his last line.

I'll pay you all back.

Light fades to black, and there is heard a final slam of jail door.

Curtain